Children's English History in Verse

Children's English History in Verse

edited by

KENNETH BAKER

faber and faber

First published in 1999
by Faber and Faber Limited
3 Queen Square London WC1N 3AU

Photoset by Parker Typesetting Service, Leicester
Printed in England by Mackays of Chatham plc, Chatham, Kent

A CIP record for this book
is available from the British Library
ISBN 0-571-19617-9

2 4 6 8 10 9 7 5 3 1

To my grandchildren,
Tess, Oonagh and Conrad

Contents

The Hanoverians, 1715–1837

The Victorian Age

The House of Windsor: England in the Twentieth Century

The Romans, the Saxons, the Vikings and the Danes

AD 43–1066

Julius Caesar invaded England in 55 BC. The Romans then returned to their province of Gaul, across the English Channel. The real invasion started under Emperor Claudius in AD 43 and the Romans controlled Britain for the next 360 years.

At the peak of its power, Rome kept a garrison of 50,000 soldiers in Britain and built a tall barrier, Hadrian's Wall, across the north of England to keep out the barbarian tribes, the Picts and the Scots.

The Romans left behind them a network of straight roads, the traces of their language – Latin – a capital called Londinium and many buildings.

The various English tribes fought among themselves and slowly three kingdoms emerged: Mercia, Northumbria and Wessex. They had to fight off invasions from the Scots and the Picts in the North and from the Vikings or Norsemen, great warriors who sailed in their longboats from Scandinavia.

In 871, Alfred became King of Wessex. The Vikings had conquered much of the country and Alfred was driven back to a small part of Somerset, the Athelney Marshes. He was determined to fight back. He built up his army, organized a network of fortified boroughs and had ships made which were longer and faster than those of the Norsemen. He succeeded in confining the Vikings to a part of North and East England, which was called the Danelaw. The Vikings, however, continued to invade England and many bloody battles were fought in the ninth and tenth centuries.

Ethelred the Unready, who succeeded to the English throne in 978, was weak and tried to buy off the invading Danes by giving them money – the famous Danegeld. Each time, the Danes asked for more, and eventually their king, Canute, became King of England in 1016. The Saxon period had come to an end and it seemed as if the country would submit to a long period of Scandinavian rule. Family rivalries, however, and the chaotic politics of the next fifty years provided an opportunity for the thrustful, well-organized and confident Normans to launch an invasion across the Channel led by William the Conqueror. For the next three hundred years the destiny of Britain was tied to that of France.

AD 61

Boadicea

When the British warrior queen,
    Bleeding from the Roman rods,
Sought, with an indignant mien,
    Counsel of her country's gods,

Sage beneath a spreading oak
    Sat the Druid, hoary chief;
Every burning word he spoke
    Full of rage, and full of grief.

'Princess! if our agèd eyes
    Weep upon thy matchless wrongs,
'Tis because resentment ties
    All the terrors of our tongues.

Rome shall perish – write that word
    In the blood that she has spilt;
Perish, hopeless and abhorred,
    Deep in ruin as in guilt.

Rome, for empire far renowned,
    Tramples on a thousand states;
Soon her pride shall kiss the ground –
    Hark! the Gaul is at her gates!

Other Romans shall arise,
    Heedless of a soldier's name;
Sounds, not arms, shall win the prize –
    Harmony the path to fame.

Then the progeny that springs
    From the forests of our land,
Armed with thunder, clad with wings,
    Shall a wider world command.

Regions Caesar never knew
    Thy posterity shall sway,

Where his eagles never flew,
  None invincible as they.'

Such the bard's prophetic words,
  Pregnant with celestial fire,
Bending, as he swept the chords
  Of his sweet but awful lyre.

She, with all a monarch's pride,
  Felt them in her bosom glow;
Rushed to battle, fought, and died;
  Dying, hurled them at the foe.

'Ruffians, pitiless as proud,
  Heaven awards the vengeance due;
Empire is on us bestowed,
  Shame and ruin wait for you.'

                                    William Cowper

In AD 60 the leader of a tribe, the Iceni, which lived in East Anglia, died and 'Roman officers plundered his kingdom; his widow, Boudicca, was flogged and his daughters raped'(Tacitus). The Iceni, led by Boudicca, rose up against the Romans and destroyed their town of Colchester but were defeated at a battle in the Midlands. A contemporary Roman, Dio, reported that the barbarians uttered loud yells but 'the Roman advance was silent and disciplined'. To avoid the humiliation of being led in triumph through Rome, Boudicca killed herself by taking poison.

c. 300

THE ROMAN OCCUPATION

from **The Roman Centurion's Song**

Legate, I had the news last night – my Cohort ordered home
By ship to Portus Itius and thence by road to Rome.
I've marched the Companies aboard, the arms are stowed
  below:
Now let another take my sword. Command me not to go!

I've served in Britain forty years, from Vectis to the Wall.
I have none other home than this, nor any life at all.
Last night I did not understand, but, now the hour draws near
That calls me to my native land, I feel that land is here.

Here where men say my name was made, here where my work
    was done,
Here where my dearest dead are laid – my wife – my wife and
    son;
Here where time, custom, grief and toil, age, memory, service,
    love,
Have rooted me in British soil. Ah, how can I remove?

Let me work here for Britain's sake – at any task you will –
A marsh to drain, a road to make or native troops to drill.
Some Western camp (I know the Pict) or granite Border keep,
Mid seas of heather derelict, where our old messmates sleep.
Legate, I come to you in tears – My Cohort ordered home!
I've served in Britain forty years. What should I do in Rome?
Here is my heart, my soul, my mind – the only life I know.
I cannot leave it all behind. Command me not to go!

Rudyard Kipling

From the year AD 200, Romans were allowed to marry Britons and the
soldier in this poem gives as one of his reasons for not returning to
Rome his wife and child who had died in Britain.

after 500

THE DEATH OF KING ARTHUR

from Idylls of the King

And slowly answered Arthur from the barge:
'The old order changeth, yielding place to new,
And God fulfils Himself in many ways,
Lest one good custom should corrupt the world.
Comfort thyself: what comfort is in me?
I have lived my life, and that which I have done

May He within Himself make pure! but thou,
If thou shouldst never see my face again,
Pray for my soul. More things are wrought by prayer
Than this world dreams of. Wherefore, let thy voice
Rise like a fountain for me night and day.
For what are men better than sheep or goats
That nourish a blind life within the brain,
If, knowing God, they lift not hands of prayer
Both for themselves and those who call them friend?
For so the whole round earth is every way
Bound by gold chains about the feet of God.
But now farewell. I am going a long way
With these thou seëst – if indeed I go
(For all my mind is clouded with a doubt) –
To the island-valley of Avilion;
Where falls not hail, or rain, or any snow,
Nor ever wind blows loudly; but it lies
Deep-meadowed, happy, fair with orchard-lawns
And bowery hollows crowned with summer sea,
Where I will heal me of my grievous wound.'

So said he, and the barge with oar and sail
Moved from the brink, like some full-breasted swan
That, fluting a wild carol ere her death,
Ruffles her pure cold plume, and takes the flood
With swarthy webs. Long stood Sir Bedivere
Revolving many memories, till the hull
Looked one black dot against the verge of dawn,
And on the mere the wailing died away.

Alfred, Lord Tennyson

In the fourth and fifth centuries small bands of Anglo-Saxons, the most famous being Hengist and Horsa, set sail from Denmark and North Germany to settle in Britain. The local inhabitants put up some resistance, and we have the name of at least one of their leaders, Ambrosius Aurelianus, who seems to have been a Roman 'staying on'. The one whom everybody knows, King Arthur, has achieved the status of a legend. The legend itself was written down after the Norman Conquest, and much later written up by Tennyson. One certain fact is that Arthur defeated the Anglo-Saxons at Badon, possibly on a hilltop near Bath, at some time in the early sixth century.

Tennyson drew upon the accounts of Geoffrey of Monmouth and Thomas Malory to recreate his ideal of Romantic chivalry. He wrote:

How much of history we have in the story of Arthur is doubtful. Let not my readers press too hard on details, whether for history or for allegory . . . He is meant to be a man who spent himself in the cause of honour, duty and self-sacrifice.

c. 870

THE VIKING INVASIONS

from **The Ballad of the White Horse**

The Northmen came about our land
   A Christless chivalry:
Who knew not of the arch or pen,
Great, beautiful half-witted men
   From the sunrise and the sea.

Misshapen ships stood on the deep
   Full of strange gold and fire,
And hairy men, as huge as sin
With horned heads, came wading in
   Through the long, low sea-mire.

Our towns were shaken of tall kings
   With scarlet beards like blood:
The world turned empty where they trod,
They took the kindly cross of God
   And cut it up for wood.

And there was death on the Emperor
   And night upon the Pope:
And Alfred, hiding in deep grass,
   Hardened his heart with hope.

A sea-folk blinder than the sea
   Broke all about his land,
But Alfred up against them bare
And gripped the ground and grasped the air,
   Staggered, and strove to stand.

He bent them back with spear and spade,
  With desperate dyke and wall,
With foemen leaning on his shield
And roaring on him when he reeled;
  And no help came at all.

He broke them with a broken sword
  A little towards the sea,
And for one hour of panting peace,
Ringed with a roar that would not cease,
With golden crown and girded fleece
  Made laws under a tree.

G. K. Chesterton

King Alfred beat the Vikings at the Battle of Edington in 878. Alfred restored Christianity and even began to convert the pagan Vikings; he encouraged the scholarship which produced the *Anglo-Saxon Chronicle*, and laid down laws enforcing loyalty to the new state. He may be said to have created the English nation and certainly deserves his title of 'Alfred the Great'.

c. 870

KING ALFRED AND THE CAKES

Where lying on the hearth to bake
By chance the cake did burn:
'What! canst thou not, thou lout,' quoth she,
'Take pains the same to turn?
But serve me such another trick,
I'll thwack thee on the snout.'
Which made the patient king, good man,
Of her to stand in doubt?

Anonymous

When Alfred took refuge in the Athelney Marshes, a rumour grew up which was later recorded as fact. It was said that he had to disguise himself as a peasant and live with a swineherd and his wife. One day,

either preoccupied with his plans or cleaning his weapons, he let some cakes burn. The wife was angry and scolded him, saying, 'Turn the loaves over so that they don't burn, for I see every day that you have a huge appetite.'

937

The Battle of Brunanburh

This year King Athelstan, ring-giver, lord
of earls, and Prince Eadmund his brother, earned
lasting battle-fame with blade-edge
at Brunanburh; son of Eadweard, they sundered
the shield-wall, shattered the linden shields
with smithied brands: as often in battle,
true to their lineage, they guarded treasure, land
and villages from all invaders. Enemies
fell, both Scot and seafarer sank
doomed; that field, blood-sluiced, grew slippery
from sun-rise – the famous radiance,
God's dazzling candle, soaring
over morning earth – to the setting of that fair
creation.
    There, many warriors, many a Scot

and war-worn North-man alike, lay
spear-pierced above his shield,
dead-beat. All day, West Saxon bands
ran down the foe, hacking the spines of fugitives
with swords rasped fine. No Mercian refused
the hard sword-play with hostile heroes,
Anlaf's shipment over the heaving waves,
fated to the fray. Five young kings
lay on that field, dead by the sword,
in the slump of death, with seven earls
of Anlaf, and a countless glut of Scots
and seamen. There, the North-men's leader
was put to flight, with few survivors,
driven to his prow, a quick escape
by galley across the gloomed sea. Also
Constantine, old hand at sword-play, fled
to his native North: the old
war-king drained of swagger, his kinsmen
and friends slain in the field, his own son
left dead of wounds. That grey-aged
veteran could no more vaunt of sword-clash
than could Anlaf. Neither had cause for laughter
among their army-remnants, as victors
after battle-clamour, strenuous combat
on that reddled turf with Eadweard's
sons. Then in nailed boats the North-men,
bleeding survivors of javelins, set sail
with sapped prides through slapping seas
to Dublin, Ireland. Likewise, both brothers,
king and prince battle-proud and boisterous,
returned to their own terrain,
the meadows of Mercia. They left the dark
raven behind, charcoal-coated, horny-beaked,
to jab that carrion, and the grey-coat eagle,
the white-tailed ravening war-hawk, to have
his will of the dead, and that grizzled wolf
of the wood.

   Never was wilder carnage
seen on this island, of soldiery sword-felled,

such as the tomes of clerics tell,
since Angles and Saxons came here seeking
the Britons across broad sea, when proud
warriors whelmed the Welsh-men, and brave
earls laid hold on this land.

translated from the Anglo-Saxon by Harold Massingham

King Athelstan of Wessex and his brother, Eadmund, who were grandsons of Alfred, fought off an invasion from the North, led by Olaf Guthfrithson, the Norse King of Dublin, Constantine, King of the Scots and Picts, and Owen, King of the Strathclyde Welsh. The defenders won at Brunanburh, and this great triumph was dutifully and beautifully recorded in the regimental magazine of the House of Alfred, the *Anglo-Saxon Chronicle*.

c. 980–1016

Danegeld

It is always a temptation to an armed and agile nation,
    To call upon a neighbour and to say:
'We invaded you last night – we are quite prepared to fight,
    Unless you pay us cash to go away.'

And this is called asking for Dane-geld,
    And the people who ask it explain
That you've only to pay 'em the Dane-geld
    And then you'll get rid of the Dane!

It is always a temptation to a rich and lazy nation,
    To puff and look important and to say:–
'Though we know we should defeat you, we have not the
        time to meet you.
    We will therefore pay you cash to go away.'

And that is called paying the Dane-geld;
    But we've proved it again and again,
That if once you have paid him the Dane-geld
    You never get rid of the Dane.

It is wrong to put temptation in the path of any nation,
    For fear they should succumb and go astray,

So when you are requested to pay up or be molested,
 You will find it better policy to say:–

'We never pay *any* one Dane-geld,
 No matter how trifling the cost,
For the end of that game is oppression and shame,
 And the nation that plays it is lost!'

Rudyard Kipling

991

from **The Battle of Maldon**

Then the brave warrior raised his spear,
gripped his shield and stepped towards a seafarer,
thus the brave earl advanced on the churl;
each had evil designs on the other.
The Viking was the quicker – he hurled his foreign spear
wounding the lord of the warriors.
Byrhtnoth broke the shaft on the edge of his shield;
the imbedded spear-head sprang out of his wound.
Then he flung his spear in fury at the proud Viking
who dared inflict such pain. His aim was skilful.
The spear split open the warrior's neck.
Thus Byrhtnoth put paid to his enemy's life.
Then he swiftly hurled a second spear
which burst the Viking's breastplate, wounding him cruelly
in the chest; the deadly point pierced his heart.
The brave earl, Byrhtnoth, was delighted at this;
he laughed out loud and gave thanks to the Lord
that such good fortune had been granted to him.
But one of the seafarers sent a sharp javelin
speeding from his hand; it pierced the body
of earl Byrhtnoth, Ethelred's brave thane.

translated from the Anglo-Saxon by Kevin Crossley-Holland

The Vikings had demanded from Byrhtnoth, the Ealdorman (Chieftain) of Essex, a sum of money as their price for moving on. When he refused to pay, a bloody battle took place at Maldon in Essex which the Vikings won, and Byrhtnoth was killed. The main weapons were the spear, the sword, the dagger and the bow, which meant that victory in hand-to-hand fighting went to the strong, the agile and the swift.

c. 1020

from King Canute

King Canute was weary-hearted; he had reigned for years a
   score,
Battling, struggling, pushing, fighting, killing much and
   robbing more;
And he thought upon his actions, walking by the wild
   seashore.

But that day a something vexed him, that was clear to old
   and young:
Thrice his grace had yawned at table, when his favourite
   gleemen sung.
Once the queen would have consoled him, but he bade her
   hold her tongue.

'Something ails my gracious master,' cried the keeper of the
   seal.
'Sure, my lord, it is the lampreys served at dinner, or the veal?'
'Pshaw!' exclaimed the angry monarch. 'Keeper, 'tis not that
   I feel.

' 'Tis the *heart*, and not the dinner, fool, that doth my rest impair:
Can a king be great as I am, prithee, and yet know no care?
Oh, I'm sick, and tired, and weary.' – Someone cried, 'The
   king's arm-chair!'

Then towards the lackeys turning, quick my lord the keeper
   nodded,
Straight the king's great chair was brought him, by two footmen
   able-bodied;
Languidly he sank into it: it was comfortably wadded.

'Leading on my fierce companions,' cried he, 'over storm and
   brine,
I have fought and I have conquered! Where was glory like to
   mine?'
Loudly all the courtiers echoed: 'Where is glory like to thine?'

'Might I stay the sun above us, good Sir Bishop?' Canute cried;
'Could I bid the silver moon to pause upon her heavenly ride?
If the moon obeys my orders, sure I can command the tide.

'Will the advancing waves obey me, bishop, if I make the sign?'
Said the bishop, bowing lowly, 'Land and sea, my lord, are
   thine.'
Canute turned towards the ocean – 'Back!' he said, 'thou
   foaming brine.

'From the sacred shore I stand on, I command thee to retreat;
Venture not, thou stormy rebel, to approach thy master's seat:
Ocean, be thou still! I bid thee come not nearer to my feet!'

But the sullen ocean answered with a louder, deeper roar,
And the rapid waves drew nearer, falling sounding on the
   shore;
Back the keeper and the bishop, back the king and courtiers
   bore.

And he sternly bade them never more to kneel to human clay,
But alone to praise and worship That which earth and seas
   obey:
And his golden crown of empire never wore he from that day.
. . . King Canute is dead and gone: parasites exist alway.

William Makepeace Thackeray

Canute, whose name was also spelt Cnut, was King of Denmark and
Norway, as well as of England from 1016 to 1035. Much of his reign was
spent in holding this large empire together. Canute's rule in England
was beneficial: he encoded the law, supported the Church and
maintained peace. He was a courageous and powerful figure whose
reign appears as a golden interlude shining through the Dark Ages.
Powerful, though not omnipotent!

The Normans and the
Plantagenets, 1066–1399

Everyone knows what happened in 1066. In that year, Edward
the Confessor, who had no children, died, and Harold, Earl of
Wessex, who had only a distant claim to the throne, quickly got
himself crowned. After beating off a rival contender, Harold of
Norway, at the Battle of Stamford Bridge in the north, he
marched south to fight off another, William, Duke of Nor-
mandy, who had a rather better claim, and to whom, moreover,
Harold had once sworn allegiance. William had landed at
Pevensey Bay in Sussex and, when the two armies met at
Hastings, Harold was killed, probably by an arrow in his eye.
His body was not given to his mother, as was customary, but at
William's command it was buried at the top of a cliff with a
stone bearing the inscription:

> By the Duke's command, O Harold, you rest here a king,
> That you may still be guardian of the shore and sea.

Three Norman kings ruled England until 1135. The Norman
Conquest was very thorough. The Domesday survey, started by
William in 1085, showed that the rental value of England was
£37,000 per year and that about 250 people with incomes of
over £100 a year in effect controlled the country. While they
were in power only 10,000 Normans lived in England, but their
grip was complete. They built castles as fortified residences for
the barons. The barons exacted loyalty from their knights, and
the knights from their peasants. The barons swore loyalty to the
King, who in return granted them the use of his land. This was
known as the feudal system and its interlocking obligations
were the foundation of English society for over 300 years.

The Norman Conquest meant that England's political destiny
was shaped not by links across the North Sea to Scandinavia but
by links across the Channel to France. The daughter of Henry I
(ruled 1100–1135), Matilda, married the Count D'Anjou, and
their son, Henry II (1154–1189), was the first of the Plantagenet
kings. He governed a vast empire that extended over Normandy,
Anjou and, through his wife Eleanor, Aquitaine. Henry II spent
most of his life in the saddle, travelling over his widespread
dominions. Even with Henry's energy, it was becoming more
and more difficult to hold this sprawling empire together. His

son, Richard I (1189–1199), also known as Richard the Lionheart, spent less than a year in England and never learnt English. His brother, John (1199–1216), lost much of Anjou and in 1259 Henry III (1216–1272), in the Treaty of Paris, renounced his claim to Henry II's inheritance. English possessions in France were then limited to a part of Gascony and Calais.

During the twelfth and thirteenth centuries, English kings tried to extend their control over parts of Britain. Edward I (1272–1307) twice invaded Wales and controlled it by building a string of castles. Known as the 'Hammer of the Scots', he insisted on being the feudal overlord of the Scottish kingdom of John Balliol. This was resisted by Robert the Bruce, and Edward I died leading an expedition against him.

During the period of the Normans and the Plantagenets, the basis of English Common Law was established by Henry I and Edward I. The Normans had introduced Old French as the official language of the country, but this slowly disappeared and the English language was fashioned and shaped, notably by Geoffrey Chaucer.

The Kings and Queens of England after the Conquest

Willie, Willie, Harry, Ste,
Harry, Dick, John, Harry 3;
1, 2, 3 Neds, Richard 2,
Harries 4, 5, 6 – then who?
Edwards 4, 5, Dick the Bad,
Harries twain, and then the lad;
Mary, Bessie, James the Vain,
Charlie, Charlie, James again;
William and Mary, Anne, and *gloria!* –
4 Georges, William and Victoria,
Ned and George; repeat again;
And then Elizabeth comes to reign.

Anonymous

William the Conqueror

1087

DEATH OF WILLIAM THE CONQUEROR

He ordered the poor to build castles.
This was very hard work.
The king was a tough man
And he took many gold coins from his people
And many more hundreds of pounds in silver . . .
This was most unfair, and he did not really need the money . . .
He marked out a huge area for deer, and made laws about it.
Anyone who killed a hart or a hind
Was to be blinded . . .
He loved the stags as dearly
As though he had been their father . . .
The rich complained and the poor wept.
But he was too merciless to care if everyone hated him.
And they just had to obey him.
Otherwise, they lost their lives and their lands
And their goods and their king's friendship.
Alas! that any man should behave in this proud way
And declare that he is so far above all other men!
May Almighty God show mercy on his soul
And pardon him his sins.

The Peterborough Chronicler

Much of our knowledge of these times comes from chronicles written
by the monks. This monk from Peterborough in fact wrote in prose, but
of a kind that suggests the rhythm of verse, and he noted both the good
things and the bad things about William's reign.

King William II, 1087–1100

1100

The Death of Rufus

To hunt rode fierce King Rufus,
Upon a holy morn –
The Church had summon'd him to pray,
But he held the Church in scorn.
Sir Walter Tyrrel rode with him,
And drew his good bow-string;
He drew the string to smite a deer,
But his arrow smote the king!

Hurl'd from his trembling charger,
The death-struck monarch lay;
While fast, as flees the startled deer,
Rash Tyrrel fled away:
On the spot where his strong hand had made
So many desolate,
He died with none to pity him –
Such was the tyrant's fate!

None mourn'd for cruel Rufus:
With pomp they buried him;
But no heart grieved beside his bier –
No kindly eye grew dim;
But poor men lifted up their heads,
And clasp'd their hands, and said:
'Thank God, the ruthless Conqueror
And his stern son are dead!'

Menella Smedley

The most memorable thing about William Rufus was his mysterious death in the New Forest. He debased the coinage, fell out with the Church and disinherited many baronial families. His chroniclers, mainly churchmen, deplored the morals of his court and lamented his oppressive regime, but he was a shrewd, successful politician who started building one of the finest civic edifices of medieval times, Westminster Hall.

King Henry II, 1154–89

1172

THE MURDER OF THOMAS À BECKET

from Murder in the Cathedral

KNIGHTS

Where is Becket, the traitor to the King?
Where is Becket, the meddling priest?
Come down Daniel to the lion's den,
Come down Daniel for the mark of the beast.

Are you washed in the blood of the Lamb?
Are you marked with the mark of the beast?
Come down Daniel to the lion's den,
Come down Daniel and join in the feast.

Where is Becket the Cheapside brat?
Where is Becket the faithless priest?
Come down Daniel to the lions' den,
Come down Daniel and join in the feast.

THOMAS

It is the just man who
Like a bold lion, should be without fear.
I am here.
No traitor to the King. I am a priest,
A Christian, saved by the blood of Christ,
Ready to suffer with my blood.
This is the sign of the church always,
The sign of blood. Blood for blood.
His blood given to buy my life,
My blood given to pay for His death,
My death for His death.

FIRST KNIGHT

Absolve all those you have excommunicated.

SECOND KNIGHT

Resign the powers you have arrogated.

THIRD KNIGHT

Restore to the King the money you appropriated.

FOURTH KNIGHT

Renew the obedience you have violated.

THOMAS

For my Lord I am now ready to die,
That his Church may have peace and liberty.
Do with me as you will, to your hurt and shame;
But none of my people, in God's name,
Whether layman or clerk, shall you touch.
This I forbid.

KNIGHTS

Traitor! traitor! traitor!

THOMAS

You, Reginald, three times traitor you;
Traitor to me as my temporal vassal,
Traitor to me as your spiritual lord,
Traitor to God in desecrating His Church.

FIRST KNIGHT

No faith do I owe to a renegade,
And what I owe shall now be paid.

T. S. Eliot

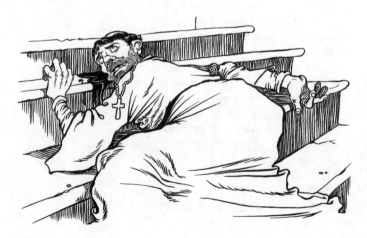

Henry II and Thomas à Becket had been close friends, but the latter, who was made Chancellor of England as well as Archbishop of Canterbury, underwent a marked change, becoming increasingly devout and aloof. He defended the power of the Catholic Church against the growing authority of Henry's state. Becket fled to France, but was then coaxed back and, after a short reconciliation with the King, was murdered in Canterbury Cathedral. Within three years he was canonized, in time becoming England's most popular saint.

Richard I 1189-99

1191

THE THIRD CRUSADE

With numberless rich pennons streaming
And flags and banners of fair seeming
Then thirty thousand Turkish troops
And more, ranged in well ordered groups,
Garbed and accoutred splendidly,
Dashed on the host impetuously.
Like lightning speed their horses fleet,
And dust rose thick before their feet.
Moving ahead of the emirs
There came a band of trumpeters
And other men with drums and tabors
There were, who had no other labours
Except upon their drums to hammer
And hoot, and shriek and make great clamour.
So loud their tabors did discord
They had drowned the thunder of the Lord.

Ambroise the Chronicler

Richard the Lionheart looked upon England as a treasure house from which to fund his campaign abroad. He spent less than a year of his reign in the country, which has earned him a splendid statue outside the Houses of Parliament. In 1190 he set out at the head of the Third Crusade with the purpose of seizing Jerusalem, recapturing a piece of wood from the Holy Cross, and, more to the point, acquiring as much gold and silver as possible. He forced the Turks' leader, Saladin, to abandon the city of Acre in Palestine. This poem describes the battle of Arsuf, a triumph for Richard, though he was unable to capture Jerusalem itself. On the way back to England, he was imprisoned in Germany and had to be ransomed. After a short spell in England in 1194, he spent the rest of his reign fighting in France. He was wounded by a bolt from a crossbow shot by a man whose shield was a frying-pan. The wound turned septic and Richard died, but not before forgiving his assailant.

King John, 1199–1216

1215

MAGNA CHARTA

The Reeds of Runnymede

At Runnymede, at Runnymede,
  What say the reeds at Runnymede?
The lissom reeds that give and take,
That bend so far, but never break.
They keep the sleepy Thames awake
  With tales of John at Runnymede.

At Runnymede, at Runnymede,
  Oh hear the reeds at Runnymede:–
'You mustn't sell, delay, deny,
A freeman's right or liberty,
It wakes the stubborn Englishry,
  We saw 'em roused at Runnymede!

'When through our ranks the Barons came,
With little thought of praise or blame,
But resolute to play the game,
  They lumbered up to Runnymede;
And there they launched in solid line,
The first attack on Right Divine –
The curt, uncompromising 'Sign!'
  That settled John at Runnymede.

'At Runnymede, at Runnymede,
  Your rights were won at Runnymede!
No freeman shall be fined or bound,
Or dispossessed of freehold ground,
Except by lawful judgment found
And passed upon him by his peers!
Forget not, after all these years,
  The Charter signed at Runnymede.'

And still when Mob or Monarch lays
Too rude a hand on English ways,
The whisper wakes, the shudder plays,
   Across the reeds at Runnymede.
And Thames, that knows the moods of kings,
And crowds and priests and suchlike things,
Rolls deep and dreadful as he brings
   Their warning down from Runnymede!

Rudyard Kipling

Unlike his brother Richard, King John lost many battles and most of the Angevin Empire in France. He was nicknamed 'Softsword' after surrendering in 1204. He tried to intimidate the over-mighty barons by keeping their sons as hostages, and he exacted high taxes from them. In 1215, on an island in the Thames at Runnymede, they replied by making him sign a list of promises which came to be known as Magna Charta. Some clauses were trivial – concerning, for instance, fish traps in the Medway – but the thirty-ninth declared: 'No free man shall be arrested, or imprisoned, or have his property taken away, or be outlawed, or exiled, or in any way ruined, except by lawful judgment . . . or by the law of the land.' Future kings of England had to swear to accept the terms of Magna Charta. Although 'King John was not a good man', one good thing he did was to proclaim that the Jews should not be persecuted.

King Henry III, 1216–72

1264

SIMON DE MONTFORT'S REBELLION

from **The Song of Lewes**

So whether it is that the King, misled
By flattering talk to giving his consent,
And truly ignorant of their designs
Unknowingly approves such wrongs as these
Whose only end can be destruction, and
The ruin of his land; or whether he,
With malice in his heart, and ill-intent,
Commits these shameful crimes by raising up
His royal state and power far beyond
The reach of all his country's laws, so that
His whim is satisfied by the abuse
Of royal privilege and strength; if thus
Or otherwise this land of ours is brought
To total rack and ruin, and at last
The kingdom is left destitute, it is
The duty of the great and noble men
To rescue it, to purge the land of all
Corruption and all false authority.

For in this year of grace, twelve sixty-four,
The feast of Good Saint Pancras four days past,
The English army rode the heavy storm
Of mighty war, at Lewes' Castle walls.
Then reason to blind fury did give way,
And life to the bright sword. They battle joined
The fourteenth day of May, and dreadful was
The strife in Sussex County, and the See
Of Chichester's Lord Bishop. Hundreds fell,
For mighty was the sword; virtue prevailed,

And evil men took to their heels and fled.
Against these wicked men, our great good Lord
Stood firm, and with the radiant shield of truth
Endued with righteous strength the pure of heart.
Routed their foes, by strength of arms without,
And craven fear within, on them did shine,
More to increase their valour, Heaven's smile.

Roger de Berksted

Henry III had accepted Magna Charta, but his reckless and extravagant behaviour as king led to bankruptcy and he resorted to arbitrary levies and taxes to make money. The nobles, with the former royal favourite Simon de Montfort at their head, sought to control Henry through regular meetings of their Council, sometimes called Parliament, but he resisted and civil war broke out. In 1264 de Montfort won a victory over the royal army at Lewes, capturing both Henry and his heir, Edward. But his success was short-lived. Several of his principal supporters found him insufferably arrogant and deserted him. Within a year he was defeated and killed at Evesham by Edward, a man of sterner stuff than his father. This poem, thought to be by a Franciscan friar, and written in Latin, gives voice to the rebels' grievances and would seem to indicate the strength of feeling against the king.

King Edward I, 1272–1307

1276

THE SUBJUGATION OF WALES

from **The Bard**

'Ruin seize thee, ruthless King!
  Confusion on thy banners wait;
Tho' fann'd by Conquest's crimson wing,
  They mock the air with idle state.
Helm, nor hauberk's twisted mail,
Nor e'en thy virtues, Tyrant shall avail
  To save thy secret soul from nightly fears,
  From Cambria's curse, from Cambria's tears!'
Such were the sounds that o'er the crested pride
  Of the first Edward scatter'd wild dismay,
As down the steep of Snowdon's shaggy side,
  He wound with toilsome march his long array.
Stout Glo'ster stood aghast in speechless trance:
'To arms!' cried Mortimer, and couch'd his quiv'ring lance.

  On a rock whose haughty brow
Frowns o'er cold Conway's foaming flood,
  Robed in the sable garb of woe,
With haggard eyes the poet stood;
(Loose his beard, and hoary hair
Stream'd, like a meteor, to the troubled air;)
And with a master's hand, and prophet's fire,
Struck the deep sorrows of his lyre.

'Hark, how each giant-oak, and desert cave,
Sighs to the torrent's awful voice beneath!
O'er thee, oh King! their hundred arms they wave,
  Revenge on thee in hoarser murmurs breathe;
Vocal no more, since Cambria's fatal day,
To high-born Hoel's harp, or soft Llewellyn's lay.

[. . .]

No more I weep. They do not sleep.
  On yonder cliffs, a grisly band,
I see them sit, they linger yet,
  Avengers of their native land:
With me in dreadful harmony they join,
  And weave with bloody hands the tissue of thy line . . .'

Thomas Gray

Thomas Gray, who lived in the eighteenth century, writes of events 600 years earlier. He describes a Welsh poet and prophet cursing the advance of Edward I's armies into Snowdonia, which had been the bastion of Welsh resistance to English rule. The cause of Llewellyn, the Welsh prince, was lost, and many great fortified castles were built to make the conquest of Wales permanent. At the most magnificent of these, Caernarvon, Edward's son was proclaimed Prince of Wales.

ROBIN HOOD

The Ballad of Robin Hood and the Bishop of Hereford

Come, gentlemen all, and listen a while;
  A story I'll to you unfold –
How Robin Hood servèd the Bishop,
  When he robb'd him of his gold.

As it befel in merry Barnsdale,
  And under the green-wood tree,
The Bishop of Hereford was to come by,
  With all his companye.

'Come, kill a ven'son,' said bold Robin Hood,
  'Come, kill me a good fat deer;
The Bishop's to dine with me to day,
  And he shall pay well for his cheer.

'We'll kill a fat ven'son,' said bold Robin Hood,
  'And dress't by the highway-side,
And narrowly watch for the Bishop,
  Lest some other way he should ride.'

He dress'd himself up in shepherd's attire,
   With six of his men also;
And the Bishop of Hereford came thereby,
   As about the fire they did go.

'What matter is this?' said the Bishop;
   'Or for whom do you make this a-do?
Or why do you kill the King's ven'son,
   When your company is so few?'

'We are shepherds,' said bold Robin Hood,
   'And we keep sheep all the year;
And we are disposed to be merry this day,
   And to kill of the King's fat deer.'

'You are brave fellowes,' said the Bishop,
   'And the King of your doings shall know;
Therefore make haste, come along with me,
   For before the King you shall go.'

'O pardon, O pardon,' says bold Robin Hood,
   'O pardon, I thee pray!
For it never becomes your lordship's coat
   To take so many lives away.'

'No pardon, no pardon!' the Bishop says;
   'No pardon I thee owe;
Therefore make haste, come along with me,
   For before the King you shall go.'

Robin set his back against a tree,
   And his foot against a thorn,
And from underneath his shepherd's coat
   He pull'd out a bugle horn.

He put the little end to his mouth,
   And a loud blast did he blow,
Till threescore and ten of bold Robin's men
   Came running all on a row;

All making obeisance to bold Robin Hood;
   – 'Twas a comely sight for to see:

'What matter, my master,' said Little John,
   'That you blow so hastilye?' –

'O here is the Bishop of Hereford,
   And no pardon we shall have.' –
'Cut off his head, master,' said Little John,
   'And throw him into his grave.' –

'O pardon, O pardon,' said the Bishop,
   'O pardon, I thee pray!
For if I had known it had been you,
   I'd have gone some other way.' –

'No pardon, no pardon!' said Robin Hood;
   'No pardon I thee owe;
Therefore make haste, come along with me,
   For to merry Barnsdale you shall go.'

Then Robin has taken the Bishop's hand
   And led him to merry Barnsdale;
He made him to stay and sup with him that night,
   And to drink wine, beer and ale.

'Call in the reckoning,' said the Bishop,
   'For methinks it grows wondrous high.' –
'Lend me your purse, Bishop,' said Little John,
   'And I'll tell you by-and-by.'

Then Little John took the Bishop's cloak,
    And spread it upon the ground,
And out of the Bishop's portmantua
    He told three hundred pound.

'So now let him go,' said Robin Hood;
    Said Little John, 'That may not be;
For I vow and protest he shall sing us a mass
    Before that he go from me.'

Robin Hood took the Bishop by the hand,
    And bound him fast to a tree,
And made him to sing a mass, God wot,
    To him and his yeomandrye.

Then Robin Hood brought him through the wood
    And caused the music to play,
And he made the Bishop to dance in his boots,
    And they set him on 's dapple-grey,
And they gave the tail within his hand –
    And glad he could so get away!

Anonymous

The legend of Robin Hood was spread by word of mouth in the Middle Ages. The first written reference dates from the 1370s, and scholars have argued over whether he lived in the reign of King John, Edward I, or Edward III. The only certainty is that he operated as an outlaw in Sherwood Forest, north of Nottingham. Over the centuries, his status as a highway robber was transformed into that of a social hero and freedom fighter. His enemies were the enemies of the common people: grasping landlords, corrupt sheriffs and corpulent clergy. Highway robbery was rife in the Middle Ages and in 1390 the poet Chaucer was pounced upon and relieved of £20. No wonder the pilgrims travelled to Canterbury in convoy. Posterity is unlikely to treat the muggers of the twentieth century so fondly.

King Edward II, 1307–27

1314

THE BATTLE OF BANNOCKBURN

Robert Bruce's March to Bannockburn

Scots, wha hae wi' Wallace bled,
  Scots, wham Bruce has aften led;
Welcome to your gory bed,
  Or to victorie.

Now's the day, and now's the hour,
See the front o' battle lower,
See approach proud Edward's power –
  Chains and slaverie!

Wha will be a traitor knave?
Wha can fill a coward's grave?
Wha sae base as be a slave?
Let him turn and flee!

Wha for Scotland's King and law,
Freedom's sword will strongly draw,
Free-man stand, or free-man fa'?
  Let him follow me!

By oppression's woes and pains!
By your sons in servile chains!
We will drain our dearest veins,
  But they shall be free!

Lay the proud usurpers low!
Tyrants fall in every foe!
Liberty's in every blow!
  Let us do, or die!

Robert Burns

In 1306, a year after Sir William Wallace, who had lead a rebellion against English rule, was beheaded, a great Scottish landowner, Robert Bruce, was crowned King of Scotland at Scone. At last a leader had emerged who could avenge his country's shameful submission to English conquest. Edward I died fighting on his way to crush Bruce's rebellion, and his son, Edward II, was decisively beaten at Bannock-burn in 1314. Bruce's armies ravaged the North of England, reaching as far as York. In 1328 the English recognized Scotland's independence, but in the following year Bruce died from leprosy leaving the kingdom to his six-year-old son, David, and his heart to an old friend, James Douglas, who took it with him on a crusade.

King Edward III, 1327–77

1348–9

THE BLACK DEATH

The Shilling in the Armpit

We see death coming into our midst like black smoke,
a plague which cuts off the young, and has no mercy for
   the fair of face.
Woe is me the shilling in the armpit:
it is seething, terrible, wherever it may come,
a white lump that gives pain and causes a loud cry,
a burden carried under the arms, a painful angry knob.
It is of the form of an apple, like the head of an onion,
a small boil that spares no one.
Great is its seething, like a burning cinder . . .

Ieuan Gethyn

The plague epidemic known as the Black Death started in Asia in the
1330s, reaching Turkey in 1347. From there it spread quickly through
Italy and France, arriving in England in 1348, and Scotland in 1349. It

lasted for only two years, although it reappeared on several occasions in England before the Great Plague of London in 1665. The bubonic plague was carried by fleas that lived on rats, and as soon as humans were bitten it became contagious. As described by this Welsh poet, boils, oozing pus and patchy blackening of the skin were symptoms of the disease. Death followed in a few days. According to some estimates, one third of the population of Europe died from it.

c. 1370

THE KNIGHTHOOD

from **The General Prologue to the Canterbury Tales**

A Knyght ther was and that a worthy man,
That fro the tyme that he first bigan
To riden out, he loved chivalrie,
Trouthe and honour, fredom and curteisie.
Ful worthy was he in his lordes werre,
And therto had he riden, no man ferre,
As wel in cristendom as in the hethenesse,
And ever honoured for his worthynesse.
At Alisaundre he was whan it was wonne;
Ful ofte tyme he hadde the bord bigonne
Aboven alle nacions in Pruce.
In Lettow had he reysed and in Ruce,
No cristen man so ofte in his degree.
In Gernade at the seege eek hadde he be
Of Algezir, and riden in Belmarye.
At Lyeys was he, and at Satalye,
Whan they were wonne; and in the Grete See
At many a noble armee hadde he be.
At mortal batailles hadde he been fiftene,
And foughten for our feith at Tramyssene
In lystes thries, and ay slayn his foo.
This ilke worthy knyght hadde been also
Somtyme with the lord of Palatye
Agayn another hethen in Turkye;
And evermoore he hadde a sovereyn prys.

And though that he were worthy, he was wys,
And of his port as meeke as is a mayde,
He never yet no vileynye ne sayde,
In al hys lyf, unto no manner wight.
He was a verray parfit, gentil knyght.

Geoffrey Chaucer

Chaucer, the Father of English Poetry, started to write in the 1360s. He had been a minor courtier, occasionally a diplomat, and for a while he was Comptroller of Customs. He lost his post in 1386 when his patron, John of Gaunt, was temporarily out of favour, and it is possible that this was when, with time on his hands, he felt he could start to put together *The Canterbury Tales*. During Edward III's reign he had been allowed a pitcher of wine every day, but this was later changed to a tun (252 wine gallons) once a year, which is what our present Poet Laureate now receives. When Chaucer died in 1400, he was buried in Westminster Abbey, the first writer to be so honoured.

The General Prologue to *The Canterbury Tales* offers a most vivid picture of some of the people who made up the England of the Middle Ages. Each portrait is precise and memorable.

THE NOBILITY

An Arundel Tomb

Side by side, their faces blurred
The earl and countess lie in stone,
Their proper habits vaguely shown
As jointed armour, stiffened pleat,
And that faint hint of the absurd –
The little dogs under their feet.

Such plainness of the pre-baroque
Hardly involves the eye, until
It meets his left-hand gauntlet, still
Clasped empty in the other; and
One sees, with a sharp tender shock,
His hand withdrawn, holding her hand.

They would not think to lie so long.
Such faithfulness in effigy
Was just a detail friends would see:

A sculptor's sweet commissioned grace
Thrown off in helping to prolong
The Latin names around the base.

They would not guess how early in
Their supine stationary voyage
The air would change to soundless damage,
Turn the old tenantry away;
How soon succeeding eyes begin
To look, not read. Rigidly they

Persisted, linked, through lengths and breadths
Of time. Snow fell, undated. Light
Each summer thronged the glass. A bright
Litter of birdcalls strewed the same
Bone-riddled ground. And up the paths
The endless altered people came,

Washing at their identity.
Now, helpless in the hollow of
An unarmorial age, a trough
Of smoke in slow suspended skeins
Above their scrap of history,
Only an attitude remains:

Time has transfigured them into
Untruth. The stone fidelity
They hardly meant has come to be
Their final blazon, and to prove
Our almost-instinct almost true:
What will survive of us is love.

Philip Larkin

the 1370s

THE POOR

from Piers Plowman

The most needy are our neighbours, if we note it well,
As prisoners in pits, and poor folk in hovels,

Charged with their children and charged by their landlords.
What they can spare from their spinning, they spend on the
    rent,
And in milk and meal, to make a mess of porridge
For the comfort of their kiddies, crying out for food.
Also they themselves suffer much in hunger,
Wasting away in winter, and waking up of nights
Rising to rock an unruly cradle,
Combing and carding wool, patching old clouts,
Rubbing and reeling yarn, and peeling their rush-lights,
That pity it is to read of it, or put it into rhyme,
The woe of these women that work in such hovels
And of many another man, ground down in grief.
Thin with thirst and hunger, yet they turn the fair side
    outward,
And are abashed to beg, lest it be acknowledged
What they need from their neighbours, at noon and at even.
Of all this I am well aware, for the world has taught me
How men are made to suffer that have many children,
With not a penny but their pittances to clothe and keep them
And many a mouth to fill, and few the pennies.
A loaf and a little ale, less than a pittance,
Cold fish or flesh, in place of roast venison,
And on Fridays and fasting-days, a farthing's worth of
    mussels
Were a feast for such folk, or a few cockles.

William Langland
translated by Nevill Coghill, 1949

The great medieval poem from which these lines come was written by a
monk from the Midlands in about the 1370s. It is full of interesting
details of the social life of the time and is one of the earliest records of
the misery that so many poor people had to endure in the Middle Ages.

King Richard II, 1377-99

1381

from The Peasants' Revolt

Tax has tenet us alle,
  probat hoc mors tot validorum,
The kyng therof hade smalle,
  fuit in manibus cupidorum;
Hit hade harde honsalle,
  dans causam fine dolorum;
Revrawnce nede most falle,
  propter peccata malorum.

In Kent this kare began,
  mox infestando potentes,
In rowte the rybawdus ran,
  sua pompis arma ferentes;
Folus dred no mon,
  regni regem neque gentes,
Churles were hor chevetan,
  vulgo pure dominantes.

Laddus loude thay loȝe,
  clamantes voce sonora,
The bisschop wen thay sloȝe,
  et corpora plura decora;
Maners down thay drowȝe,
  in regno non meliora;
Harme thay dud inoȝe,
  habuerunt libera lora.

Owre kyng hadde no rest,
  alii latuere caverna,
To ride he was ful prest,
  recolendo gesta paterna;

Jak Straw down he kest
Smythfield virtute superna.
Lord, as thou may best,
regem defende guberna.

Anonymous

This is the only poem about the Peasants' Revolt that we know was by a contemporary. With a little poetic licence, and omitting the Latin, I have made a modern English version of it that preserves something of the effect of the abrupt rhyming lines of the original:

Tax has hit us all;
The King's revenue is small;
It bears hard on us all;
Reverence now must fall.

In Kent this trouble began:
In riot the rebels ran,
For fools fear no man.
Churls were their chieftain.

Loud the lads did bray,
When the bishop they did slay.
Manors they burnt in a day –
Harm that won't go away.

Our King had no rest;
To ride forth he was pressed.
Jack Straw was a pest.
May his Majesty be blessed!

The Peasants' Revolt was the first large-scale popular uprising in English history. It started in Kent and was led by a priest, John Ball, together with Jack Straw and Wat Tyler. They protested against a poll tax of a shilling a head which was levied to pay for England's failure in the French wars. The peasants marched from Kent pillaging manors along the way and, as they advanced on London, they killed the Treasurer and the Archbishop of Canterbury.

The young king Richard II issued letters of pardon and rode out to meet the rebel forces at Smithfield. When Jack Straw and Wat Tyler approached the King, the Lord Mayor of London, Sir William Walworth, struck off Tyler's head. The mob was leaderless and the King rode among them saying, 'Sirs, will you shoot your own King? I will be your Captain.'

The following is a very short poem ascribed to John Ball:

When Adam delved
And Eve span
Who was then
The Gentleman?

Ball preached an early form of Communism and caught the nobles
and yeoman farmers on the hop. He was hanged, drawn and quartered
and his remains put on show around the country.

1399

THE STATE OF ENGLAND

from **King Richard the Second**

ACT II. *Scene* I.
London. A Room in Ely House.

GAUNT *on a couch; the* DUKE OF YORK, *and others, standing by him.*

GAUNT
Methinks, I am a prophet new inspired;
And thus, expiring, do foretell of him:
His rash fierce blaze of riot cannot last;
For violent fires soon burn out themselves:
Small showers last long, but sudden storms are short;
He tires betimes, that spurs too fast betimes;
With eager feeding, food doth choke the feeder,
Light vanity, insatiate cormorant,
Consuming means, soon preys upon itself.
This royal throne of kings, this scepter'd isle,
This earth of majesty, this seat of Mars,
This other Eden, demi-paradise;
This fortress, built by nature for herself
Against infection, and the hand of war;
This happy breed of men, this little world;
This precious stone set in the silver sea,
Which serves it in the office of a wall,
Or as a moat defensive to a house,
Against the envy of less happier lands;

This blessed plot, this earth, this realm, this England,
This nurse, this teeming womb of royal kings,
Fear'd by their breed, and famous by their birth,
Renowned for their deeds as far from home,
(For Christian service, and true chivalry,)
As is the sepulchre in stubborn Jewry,
Of the world's ransom, blessed Mary's son:
This land of such dear souls, this dear dear land,
Dear for her reputation through the world,
Is now leased out, (I die pronouncing it,)
Like to a tenement, or pelting farm:
England, bound in with the triumphant sea,
Whose rocky shore beats back to the envious siege
Of watery Neptune, is now bound in with shame,
With inky blots, and rotten parchment bonds;
That England, that was wont to conquer others,
Hath made a shameful conquest of itself:
O, would the scandal vanish with my life,
How happy then were my ensuing death!

William Shakespeare

John of Gaunt was Edward III's third son and virtually ran the country
as Regent during his father's old age and the early years of Richard II,
his nephew, who was only nine years old when he became King. John
of Gaunt was the most powerful noble in England, having been granted
the Duchy of Lancaster in 1362. He staunchly supported Richard II.
After that king's death in 1399 his son, Henry Bolingbroke, seized the
throne and reigned as Henry IV.

THE DEPOSITION OF RICHARD II

from **King Richard the Second**

ACT IV. *Scene 1.*
Westminster Hall.
BOLINGBROKE *in Council with the Lords and Commons.*
Re-enter YORK, *with* KING RICHARD, *and* OFFICERS
bearing the crown, etc.

KING RICHARD

Alack, why am I sent for to a king,
Before I have shook off the regal thoughts
Wherewith I reign'd? I hardly yet have learn'd
To insinuate, flatter, bow, and bend my knee; –
Give sorrow leave a while to tutor me
To this submission. Yet I will remember
The favours of these men: Were they not mine?
Did they not sometimes cry, All hail! to me?
So Judas did to Christ: but he, in twelve,
Found truth in all but one; I, in twelve thousand none.
God save the king! – Will no man say Amen?
Am I both priest and clerk? well then, Amen.
God save the king! although I be not he;
And yet, Amen, if Heaven do think him me. –
To do what service am I sent for hither?

YORK

To do that office, of thine own good will,
Which tired majesty did make thee offer, –
The resignation of thy state and crown
To Henry Bolingbroke.

KING RICHARD

Give me the crown: – Here, cousin, seize the crown;
Here, on this side, my hand; on that side, thine.
Now is this golden crown like a deep well,
That owes two buckets filling one another;
The emptier ever dancing in the air,
The other down, unseen, and full of water:
The bucket down, and full of tears, am I,
Drinking my griefs, whilst you mount up on high.

HENRY BOLINGBROKE

I thought you had been willing to resign.

KING RICHARD

My crown I am; but still my griefs are mine:
You may my glories and my state depose,
But not my griefs; still am I king of those.

HENRY BOLINGBROKE

Part of your cares you give me with your crown.

KING RICHARD

Your cares set up, do not pluck my cares down.
My care is – loss of care, by old care done;
Your care is – gain of care, by new care won;
The cares I give, I have, though given away;
They tend the crown, yet still with me they stay.

HENRY BOLINGBROKE

Are you contented to resign the crown?

KING RICHARD

Ay, no; – no, ay: for I must nothing be;
Therefore no no, for I resign to thee.
Now mark me how I will undo myself –
I give this heavy weight from off my head,
And this unwieldy sceptre from my hand,
The pride of kingly sway from out my heart;
With mine own tears I wash away my balm,
With mine own hand I give away my crown,
With mine own tongue deny my sacred state,
With mine own breath release all duteous oaths:
All pomp and majesty I do forswear;
My manors, rents, and revenues, I forego;
My acts, decrees, and statutes, I deny;
God pardon all oaths, that are broke to me!
God keep all vows unbroke, are made to thee!
Make me, that nothing have, with nothing grieved;
And thou with all pleased, that hast all achieved
Long may'st thou live in Richard's seat to sit,
And soon lie Richard in an earthly pit!
God save King Henry, unking'd Richard says,
And send him many years of sunshine days! –
What more remains?

William Shakespeare

Richard II's reign was dominated by a struggle between the King, the nobility and Parliament. Richard did not want his power restricted but the nobles imposed their will on him in 1388. He planned his revenge in 1397 by seizing the land of some of the great nobles and exiling them. On the death of his uncle, John of Gaunt, in 1399, he seized the lands of Gaunt's son, Henry of Lancaster (Bolingbroke), who was exiled to France. Richard II was deserted by his nobles and loathed by the merchants for his forced loans. Henry then took the opportunity of Richard's absence in Ireland to return to England and seize the throne, which he claimed by right of descent, vindicated by conquest.

The thirty-three-year-old Richard, the last of the Plantagenets, was taken to Pontefract Castle in 1400 where he was either starved to death or suffocated. Henry held a solemn requiem mass for Richard at St Paul's Cathedral.

Lancaster and York, 1399–1485

In medieval England, it was important for the king to be strong. Henry IV was a decisive leader and when he deposed Richard II it seemed possible that there might be a period of peace and prosperity. However, his son, Henry V, another strong leader, spent much of his reign winning back the lands lost in France. He died of dysentery in France in 1422 and left his empire to his one-year-old son, Henry VI. Once again England lacked a strong king.

By 1453, after a series of humiliating defeats, English authority was limited to a small part of Gascony and Calais. The barons returned to England to fight over their own lands. The two rival factions of Lancaster and York each took a rose as their symbol – red and white respectively. Their continuing battles from 1455 to 1487 became known as the War of the Roses.

Henry VI suffered from a strange malady which involved complete amnesia and extreme inertia. He simply could not rule. In 1454 Richard, Duke of York, was created Protector of the Realm, but when Henry recovered slightly in 1455, his wife, Margaret of Anjou, plotted to get rid of the Duke of York. This precipitated the Wars of the Roses. Henry VI was a passive onlooker and was deposed in 1461 by the Yorkist, Edward IV. In 1471 Henry was briefly restored to the throne by Warwick the Kingmaker but was murdered soon after. The strife continued until Richard III, the famous hunchback and the last of the Yorkists, was defeated at the Battle of Bosworth by Henry Tudor in 1485.

The records, chronicles and letters on which our knowledge of these wars are based have been supplemented by Shakespeare's plays, *Henry V, Henry VI* and *Richard III*, which were written one hundred years after the events they cover. As Elizabeth I was a direct descendant of Henry VII, the heroes are the Lancastrians. The clear message was that as Tudor rule had brought an end to bloody warfare, it was important to support loyally the authority of the Crown, for it was all too easy to slip back into anarchy and savagery.

King Henry V, 1413–22

1415

from The Battle of Agincourt

Fair stood the wind for France
When we our sails advance,
Nor now to prove our chance
    Longer will tarry;
But putting to the main,
At Caux, the mouth of Seine,
With all his martial train
    Landed King Harry.

And taking many a fort,
Furnished in warlike sort,
Marcheth towards Agincourt
    In happy hour;
Skirmishing day by day
With those that stopped his way,
Where the French general lay
    With all his power;

And turning to his men,
Quoth our brave Henry then,
'Though they to one be ten,
    Be not amazèd;
Yet have we well begun,
Battles so bravely won
Have ever to the sun
    By fame been raisèd.

'Poitiers and Cressy tell,
When most their pride did swell,
Under our swords they fell;
    No less our skill is
Than when our grandsire great,
Claiming the regal seat,

By many a warlike feat
    Lopped the French lilies.'

They now to fight are gone,
Armour on armour shone,
Drum now to drum did groan,
    To hear was wonder:
That with the cries they make
The very earth did shake;
Trumpet to trumpet spake,
    Thunder to thunder.

Well it thine age became,
O noble Erpingham,
Which didst the signal aim
    To our hid forces!
When, from a meadow by,
Like a storm suddenly
The English archery
    Struck the French horses:

With Spanish yew so strong,
Arrows a cloth-yard long,
That like to serpents stung,
    Piercing the weather;
None from his fellow starts,
But, playing manly parts,
And like true English hearts,
    Stuck close together.

When down their bows they threw,
And forth their bilbos drew,
And on the French they flew,
    Not one was tardy;
Arms were from shoulders sent,
Scalps to the teeth were rent,
Down the French peasants went:
    Our men were hardy.

This while our noble King,
His broad sword brandishing,

Down the French host did ding
        As to o'erwhelm it;
And many a deep wound lent,
His arms with blood besprent,
And many a cruel dent
        Bruisèd his helmet.

Upon Saint Crispin's day
Fought was this noble fray,
Which fame did not delay
        To England to carry;
Oh, when shall English men
With such acts fill a pen?
Or England breed again
        Such a King Harry?
                    Michael Drayton

from **King Henry the Fifth**

ACT IV. *Scene III.*
The English camp.

KING HENRY

This day is call'd the feast of Crispian:
He that outlives this day, and comes safe home,
Will stand a tip-toe when this day is nam'd,
And rouse him at the name of Crispian.
He that shall live this day, and see old age,
Will yearly on the vigil feast his neighbours,
And say, 'To-morrow is Saint Crispian':
Then will he strip his sleeve and show his scars,
And say, 'These wounds I had on Crispin's day.'
Old men forget: yet all shall be forgot,
But he'll remember with advantages
What feats he did that day. Then shall our names,
Familiar in his mouth as household words,
Harry the king, Bedford and Exeter,
Warwick and Talbot, Salisbury and Gloucester,
Be in their flowing cups freshly remember'd.
This story shall the good man teach his son;

And Crispin Crispian shall ne'er go by,
From this day to the ending of the world,
But we in it shall be remembered;
We few, we happy few, we band of brothers;
For he to-day that sheds his blood with me
Shall be my brother; be he ne'er so vile
This day shall gentle his condition:
And gentlemen in England, now a-bed
Shall think themselves accurs'd they were not here,
And hold their manhoods cheap whiles any speaks
That fought with us upon Saint Crispin's day.

William Shakespeare

Henry V was determined to reclaim for England the old Angevin Empire in France, and in 1415 he set sail with 1,500 ships and 10,000 fighting men. But death in battle and dysentery soon reduced this to 6,000. Withdrawing to the coast, this small army met a much larger French one and, through Henry's personal inspiration and skilful use of the long bow, defeated it at Agincourt. After that England was committed to a ruinously expensive war on the Continent: in 1418 alone the army ordered one million goose feathers to make arrow flights. In 1420 Henry married Catherine of Valois and became the heir to the French throne. From England's point of view, that represented the high point of the Hundred Years War between England and France, and from then on it was downhill all the way until at last Mary Tudor lost Calais in 1558. Henry died in 1422, from dysentery caught on the campaign, and he made the unforgivable mistake, for a medieval king, of leaving an heir just one year old.

1420

DICK WHITTINGTON'S THIRD TERM AS LORD MAYOR OF LONDON

Here must I tell the praise
    Of worthy Whittington,
Known to be in his age
    Thrice Mayor of London.
But of poor parentage

Born was he, as we hear,
And in his tender age
    Bred up in Lancashire.

Poorly to London then
    Came up this simple lad,
Where with a merchant-man,
    Soon he a dwelling had;
And in a kitchen placed
    A scullion for to be,
Whereas long time he past
    In labour drudgingly.

His daily service was
    Turning spits at the fire;
And to scour pots of brass,
    For a poor scullion's hire.
Meat and drink all his pay,
    Of coin he had no store;
Therefore to run away,
    In secret thought he bore.

So from this merchant-man
    Whittington secretly
Towards his country ran,
    To purchase liberty.

But as he went along,
  In a fair summer's morn
London bells sweetly rung,
  'Whittington, back return!'

Evermore sounding so,
  'Turn again Whittington:
For thou in time shall grow
  Lord-Mayor of London . . .'
Whereupon back again
  Whittington came with speed.
A 'prentice to remain,
  As the Lord had decreed.

But see his happy chance!
  This scullion had a cat,
Which did his state advance,
  And by it wealth he gat.
His master ventured forth,
  To a land far unknown,
With merchandise of worth,
  As is in stories shown.

Whittington had no more
  But this poor cat as than,
Which to the ship he bore,
  Like a brave merchant-man,
'Venturing the same,' quoth he,
  'I may get store of gold,
And Mayor of London be;
  As the bells have me told.'

Whittington's merchandise
  Carried was to a land
Troubled with rats and mice,
  As they did understand.
The king of that country there,
  As he at dinner sat,
Daily remained in fear
  Of many a mouse and rat.

Meat that on trenchers lay,
    No way they could keep safe;
But by rats borne away,
    Fearing no wand or staff.
Whereupon soon they brought
    Whittington's nimble cat;
Which by the king was bought;
    Heaps of gold given for that.

Home again came these men
    With their ships loaden so,
Whittington's wealth began
    By this cat thus to grow.

Scullion's life he forsook
    To be a merchant good,
And soon began to look
    How well his credit stood.

After that he was chose
    Sheriff of the city here,
And then full quickly rose
    Higher, as did appear.
For to this cities praise,
    Sir Richard Whittington
Came to be in his day,
    Thrice Mayor of London.
                    Anonymous

Dick Whittington was a wealthy silk merchant who first became Lord
Mayor of London in 1397, and again in 1406 and 1420. He was so rich
that he made loans to the Crown, for which he was rewarded by Henry
IV with a licence to ship wool from London without paying the heavy
export duty. When he died childless in 1423, his great wealth went to St
Bartholomew's Hospital and to other charities. His cat and his early
poverty were both added to his story later in the seventeenth century.

King Henry VI, 1422–1471

1436

from Plea for a Navy

The trewe processe of Englysh polycye
  Of utterwarde to kepe thys regne in rest
Of oure England, that no man may denye,
  Nere says of soth but one of the best
  Is thys, that who seith southe, northe, est, and west,
Cheryshe marchandyse, kepe thamyralté
That we bee masteres of the narowe see.

Where bene oure shippes? where bene oure swerdes become?
  Owre enmyes bid for the shippe sette a shepe.
Allas! oure reule halteth, hit is benome;
  Who dare weel say that lordeshyppe shulde take kepe?
  I wolle asaye, thoughe myne herte gynne to wepe,
To do thys werke, yf we wole ever the,
Ffor verry shame, to kepe aboute the see.

Anonymous

During Henry VI's youth from 1422 to 1437, the government of the country and the conduct of the war were in the hands of his uncles and Cardinal Beaufort. The French were inspired by Joan of Arc in 1429 and began to win back the lands conquered by England. Paris was lost in 1436, and this poem pleads for more ships to defend the country's trade, but the decline could not be stopped and in 1453 the Hundred Years War came to an end.

King Edward IV, 1461–1483

THE WARS OF THE ROSES, 1455–1487

from **Henry VI, Part I**

ACT II. *Scene IV.*
London. The Temple Garden.

SOMERSET

Judge you, my Lord of Warwick, then,
    between us.

WARWICK

Between two hawks, which flies the higher pitch;
Between two dogs, which hath the deeper mouth;
Between two blades, which bears the better temper;
Between two horses, which doth bear him best;
Between two girls, which hath the merriest eye;
I have perhaps, some shallow spirit of judgment;
But in these nice sharp quillets of the law,
Good faith, I am no wiser than a daw.

PLANTAGENET

Tut, tut! here is a mannerly forbearance:
The truth appears so naked on my side,
That any purblind eye may find it out.

SOMERSET

And on my side it is so well apparell'd,
So clear, so shining, and so evident,
That it will glimmer through a blind man's eye.

PLANTAGENET

Since you are tongue-tied, and so loath to speak,
In dumb significants proclaim your thoughts:
Let him that is a true-born gentleman,
And stands upon the honour of his birth,
If he suppose that I have pleaded truth,
From off this brier pluck a white rose with me.

SOMERSET

Let him that is no coward nor no flatterer,

But dare maintain the party of the truth,
Pluck a red rose from off this thorn with me.

WARWICK

I love no colours, and, without all colour
Of base insinuating flattery
I pluck this white rose with Plantagenet.

SUFFOLK

I pluck this red rose with young Somerset:
And say withal I think he held the right.

VERNON

Stay, lords and gentlemen, and pluck no more,
Till you conclude that he, upon whose side
The fewest roses are cropp'd from the tree,
Shall yield the other in the right opinion.

SOMERSET

Good Master Vernon, it is well objected:
If I have fewest I subscribe in silence.

PLANTAGENET

And I.

VERNON

Then for the truth and plainness of the case,
I pluck this pale and maiden blossom here,
Giving my verdict on the white rose side.

SOMERSET

Prick not your finger as you pluck it off,
Lest bleeding you do paint the white rose red,
And fall on my side so, against your will.

William Shakespeare

This meeting in the Temple Gardens in London between the two sides, romantically depicted by Shakespeare, probably never took place. But, in history, it is often what people like to believe that survives. Richard Plantagenet, Duke of York, had a claim to the throne through his uncle, who was a descendant of Edward III. He plucks a white rose. Somerset was a grandson of Edward III: he plucks a red rose. Warwick chose first the white rose and helped Edward IV to the throne, but he later abandoned Edward and brought Henry VI back to the throne. First white and then red – and for this he was called the Kingmaker.

1478

THE MURDER OF THE DUKE OF CLARENCE

from **King Richard the Third**

ACT I. *Scene IV.*
London. The Tower.

SECOND MURDERER

Make peace with God, for you must die, my lord.

CLARENCE

Have you that holy feeling in thy soul,
To counsel me to make my peace with God,
And art thou yet to thy own soul so blind,
That thou wilt war with God by murdering me?
O! sirs, consider, they that set you on
To do this deed will hate you for the deed.

SECOND MURDERER

What shall we do?

CLARENCE

Relent and save your souls.

FIRST MURDERER

Relent! 'tis cowardly and womanish.

CLARENCE

Not to relent, is beastly, savage, devilish.
Which of you, if you were a prince's son,
Being pent from liberty, as I am now,
If two such murderers as yourselves came to you,
Would not entreat for life?
My friend, I spy some pity in thy looks;
O! if thine eye be not a flatterer,
Come thou on my side, and entreat for me,
As you would beg, were you in my distress:
A begging prince what beggar pities not?

SECOND MURDERER

Look behind you, my lord.

FIRST MURDERER

Take that, and that:

(Stabs him.)
If all this will not do,
I'll drown you in the malmsey-butt within.
(Exit, with the body.)
William Shakespeare

If the Duke of Clarence had not met his end in a butt of malmsey wine, his death would no doubt have been forgotten amid the baronial mayhem of the fifteenth century. He was a younger brother of Edward IV and was ambitious but unstable. He supported Warwick the Kingmaker during his rebellion of 1469–71, but upon Edward's return from exile in 1471 defected back to his brother and fought alongside him at Barnet and Tewkesbury. Although restored to favour, he was never satisfied with his power, and in 1478 Edward had him arrested for high treason. Tradition relates that he was executed by being drowned in his favourite wine. Shakespeare made Richard of Gloucester his murderer, but there is no external evidence for this and the full responsibility must lie with Edward.

King Edward V, 1483, and King Richard III, 1483–5

THE MURDER OF THE PRINCES IN THE TOWER

from **King Richard the Third**

ACT IV. *Scene III.*
London. A Room of State in the Palace.
(*Enter* TYRREL)

TYRREL

The tyrannous and bloody act is done;
The most arch deed of piteous massacre,
That ever yet this land was guilty of,
Dighton, and Forrest, whom I did suborn
To do this piece of ruthless butchery,
Albeit they were flesh'd villains, bloody dogs,
Melting with tenderness and mild compassion,
Wept like two children, in their death's sad story.
O thus, quoth Dighton, *lay the gentle babes, –*
Thus, thus, quoth Forrest, *girdling one another*
Within their alabaster innocent arms:
Their lips were four red roses on a stalk,
Which, in their summer beauty, kiss'd each other.
A book of prayers on their pillow lay;
Which once, quoth Forrest, *almost changed my mind:*
But, O, the devil – there the villain stopp'd;
When Dighton thus told on, – *we smothered*
The most replenished sweet work of nature.
That, from the prime creation e'er she framed. –
Hence both are gone with conscience and remorse,
They could not speak; and so I left them both,
To bear this tidings to the bloody king:
And here he comes.

        (*Enter* KING RICHARD)
        All health, my sovereign lord!

KING RICHARD
  Kind Tyrrel! am I happy in thy news?
                              William Shakespeare

In April 1483 Edward IV died and was succeeded by his twelve-year-old son, Edward V, whose coronation was planned for 22 June. Richard of Gloucester, Edward IV's brother and the young King's uncle, was made Protector. He realized that the Woodville family, relations of Edward, would wait until the King came of age and then turn upon Richard himself. So he moved quickly to place Edward and his younger brother under guard in the Tower of London, an act which had the full support of the Archbishop of Canterbury, and after that they disappeared. With that accomplished, he claimed the throne and was crowned in July. Tudor propaganda accused him of suffocating the princes in the Tower; of killing Henry VI; and of having his brother, the Duke of Clarence, murdered. So bad was his reputation that he was obliged personally to deny that he had done away with his wife, Anne, in order to marry his niece.

1485

THE BATTLE OF BOSWORTH

from **King Richard the Third**

ACT V. *Scene IV.*
Another part of the field.
Alarum; excursions. Enter NORFOLK *and forces fighting;*
to him CATESBY.

CATESBY
  Rescue, my Lord of Norfolk, rescue, rescue!
  The King enacts more wonders than a man,
  Daring an opposite to every danger:
  His horse is slain, and all on foot he fights,
  Seeking for Richmond in the throat of death.
  Rescue, fair lord, or else the day is lost!
              (*Alarums. Enter* KING RICHARD)
KING RICHARD
  A horse! a horse! my kingdom for a horse!

CATESBY

Withdraw, my lord; I'll help you to a horse.

KING RICHARD

Slave, I have set my life upon a cast,
And I will stand the hazard of the die.
I think there be six Richmonds in the field;
Five have I slain to-day instead of him.
A horse! a horse! my kingdom for a horse!   [*Exeunt.*]
    Another part of the field.

Alarum. Enter KING RICHARD *and* RICHMOND; *they fight.*
RICHARD *is slain. Retreat and flourish. Re-enter* RICHMOND,
    DERBY *bearing the crown, with divers other Lords.*

RICHMOND

God and your arms be praised, victorious friends!
The day is ours; the bloody dog is dead.

DERBY

Courageous Richmond, well hast thou acquit thee.
Lo, here, this long usurped royalty
From the dead temples of this bloody wretch
Have I pluck'd off, to grace thy brows withal;
Wear it, enjoy it, and make much of it.

RICHMOND

O now, let Richmond and Elizabeth,
The true succeeders of each royal house,
By God's fair ordinance conjoin together;
And let their heirs, (God, if thy will be so,)
Enrich the time to come with smooth-faced peace,
With smiling plenty, and fair prosperous days;
Now civil wounds are stopp'd, peace lives again:
That she may long live here, God say – Amen.

    [*Exeunt.*]
    William Shakespeare

Richard was feared and detested by many of the noble families. In
August 1485 Henry Tudor, Earl of Richmond, landed at Milford Haven,
and within three weeks was King. So ended Richard III's reign. Some
historians have tried to defend his reputation, but it is no easy task to
contradict Shakespeare.

The Tudors, 1485–1603

Under the Tudors England became a nation state. Henry VII established an efficient administrative system; Henry VIII, thwarted in getting a divorce by the Pope, broke from Catholic Rome and created the Church of England; his eldest daughter Mary failed to reinstate Catholicism; and his younger daughter Elizabeth became the symbol of a proud and defiant country which could take on and defeat the power of Spain, the greatest empire in the world, ruled by Philip II.

When the power of the Catholic Church was destroyed, its wealth was distributed through the Dissolution of the Monasteries. The nobles and middle classes who obtained these lands made sure that the clock was not going to be turned back to Rome. Throughout the Tudor period the merchant classes gained more influence and power, notably through Parliament, which was Henry VIII's chosen instrument to establish the Church of England. The Act of Supremacy of 1534, which made the King the Supreme Head of the Church of England, was an act passed by Parliament.

Elizabeth used Parliament reluctantly, but its approval was needed for the raising of taxes. Elizabeth was prudent with the nation's resources and was able to borrow money from the Netherlands to finance her wars with Spain at a far better rate than that which the Spaniards had to pay. In her reign, sailors like Drake, Ralegh, Gilbert, Grenville and Hawkins turned England into a seafaring nation whose ships traded in the West Indies, America, Africa and the East Indies – the beginnings of the Empire were established.

At the end of the Tudor period, there was a great cultural outburst and its star of genius was William Shakespeare. More than any other writer, he helped to fashion the English language which, in Elizabeth's reign, was spoken by about 5 million people and which, today, is spoken by over 750 million people across the world.

King Henry VII, 1485–1509

THE TUDOR ROSE

'I loue the rose both red & white.'
'Is that your pure perfite appetite?'
'To here talke of them is my delite!'
'Ioyed may we be,
oure prince to se,
& rosys thre!'

Anonymous

Henry Tudor, of the red rose of Lancaster, married Elizabeth, daughter of Edward IV, of the white rose of York, and thereby brought the dynastic Wars of the Roses to an end. The resulting hybrid, the Tudor rose, the third alluded to here, was personified in the figure of Arthur, Henry's heir, who, however, died young, leaving the succession to his brother, Henry VIII.

King Henry VIII, 1509–47

HENRY'S WIVES

Divorced, beheaded, died,
Divorced, beheaded, survived.

Anonymous

This little poem describes the fate of each of the six wives of Henry VIII:
Catherine of Aragon, Anne Boleyn, Jane Seymour, Anne of Cleves,
Catherine Howard, and Catherine Parr.

c. 1510

A TUDOR TEXTILE FACTORY

from The Pleasant History of Jack of Newbury

Within one roome, being large and long
There stood two hundred Loomes full strong.
Two hundred men, the truth is so,
Wrought in the Loomes all in a row.
By every one a pretty boy
Sate making quilts with mickle joy,
And in another place hard by
A hundred women merrily
Were carding hard with joyful cheere
Who singing sate with voyces cleere,
And in a chamber close beside
Two hundred maidens did abide,
In petticoats of Stammell red,
And milk white kerchiefs on their head.
Their smocke-sleeves like to winter snow
That on the Westerne mountaines flow,
And each sleeve with a silken band
Was featly tied at the hand.

These pretty maids did never lin
But in that place all day did spin,
And spinning so with voyces meet
Like nightingales they sang full sweet.
Then to another roome, came they
Where children were in poore aray;
And every one sate picking wool
The finest from the course to cull:
The number was sevenscore and ten
The children of poore silly men:
And these their labours to requite
Had every one a penny at night,
Beside their meat and drinke all day,
Which was to them a wondrous stay.
Within another place likewise

Full fifty proper men he spies
And these were sheremen everyone,
Whose skill and cunning there was showne:
And hardy by them there did remaine
Full four-score rowers taking paine.
A Dye-house likewise had he then,
Wherein he kept full forty men:
And likewise in his Fulling Mill
Full twenty persons kept he still.

Thomas Deloney

Thomas Deloney was a Tudor poet. This poem was written in 1597 and achieved great popularity. It celebrates a legendary figure of the Tudor cloth industry, John Winchcombe, who lived in the reign of Henry VIII and, among other things, led one hundred of his apprentices into battle at Flodden Field in 1513. The manufacture of cloth was the major economic activity of Tudor England. In the Middle Ages the various processes involved in the making of cloth were organized by separate trade associations known as guilds. In the sixteenth century, rich merchants began the practice of gathering the various trades under a single roof, and weavers regularly petitioned Parliament against this early movement towards capitalism.

Cardinal Wolsey's Ascendancy, 1515–1529

> Begot by butchers
> But by Bishops bred
> How high his honour
> Hold his haughty head.
>
> *Anonymous*

The son of an Ipswich butcher, Thomas Wolsey more or less ran the country in the early years of Henry's reign. As a Cardinal, Archbishop of York, and Lord Chancellor of England, he lived in sumptuous style, the envy of the nobility and, eventually, of the King himself. He dined off of gold plates, had his red hat carried before him, and built Hampton Court. But he failed, when required, to obtain for his master a divorce from Catherine of Aragon. He fell from grace and was arrested, but died while being taken to be tried in London.

1518

THE FRENCH FASHION OF THE ENGLISH GALLANT

> He struts about
> In cloaks of fashion French. His girdle, purse,
> And sword are French. His hat is French.

His nether limbs are cased in French costume.
His shoes are French. In short, from top to toe
He stands the Frenchman.

With accent French he speaks the Latin tongue,
With accent French the tongue of Lombardy,
To Spanish words he gives an accent French,
German he speaks with his same accent French,
In truth he seems to speak with accent French,
All but the French itself. The French he speaks
With accent British.

translated from the Latin of Thomas More

Henry VIII admired French clothes and French manners, and he made French the language of his courtiers. Thomas More, in a Latin poem, pointed out the pointlessness of this attempted conversion, all the more untimely when the national consciousness of England was being formed through the break from Rome, and William Tyndale was about to start his translation of the Bible into English.

c. 1510

TUDOR FOOTBALL

Eche time and season hath his delite and joyes,
Loke in the stretes, behold the little boyes,
Howe in fruite season for joy they sing and hop,
In Lent is each one full busy with his top
And nowe in winter for all the greevous colde
All rent and ragged a man may them beholde,
They have great pleasour supposing well to dine,
When men be busied in killing of fat swine,
They get the bladder and blowe it great and thin,
With many beanes or peason put within,
It ratleth, soundeth, and shineth clere and fayre,
While it is throwen and caste up in the ayre,
Eche one contendeth and hath a great delite
With foote and with hande the bladder for to smite,
If it fall to grounde, they lifte it up agayne,

This wise to labour they count it for no payne,
Renning and leaping they drive away the colde,
The sturdie plowmen lustie, strong and bolde
Ouercommeth the winter with driving the foote-ball,
Forgetting labour and many a grevous fall.

Alexander Barclay

THE KING'S PLEASURES

The Hunt is Up

The hunt is up, the hunt is up,
And it is well nigh day;
And Harry our King is gone hunting
To bring his deer to bay.

The east is bright with morning light,
And darkness it is fled,
The merry horn wakes up the morn
To leave his idle bed.

The horses snort to be at the sport,
The dogs are running free,
The woods rejoice at the merry noise
Of hay-taranta-tee-ree.

The sun is glad to see us clad
All in our lusty green,
And smiles in the sky as he rideth high
To see and to be seen.

Awake all men, I say again
Be merry as you may:
For Harry our king is gone hunting
To bring his deer to bay.

Anonymous

The most extrovert of English kings, Henry VIII threw himself into
vigorous physical activity of all kinds. The chronicler Edward Hall
noted that, during a royal progress in 1511, the King indulged 'in
shooting, singing, dancing, wrestling, casting the bar, playing at the

recorders, flute and virginals, and in setting of songs and making of ballads, and did set two godly masses'. He spent many days of his life in the saddle. In 1524 he was almost killed in a joust with the Duke of Suffolk.

1535

THE EXECUTION OF SIR THOMAS MORE

Sir Thomas More

Holbein's More, my patron saint as a convert,
the gold chain of S's, the golden rose,
the plush cap, the brow's damp feathertips of hair,
the good eyes' stern, facetious twinkle, ready
to turn from executioner to martyr –
or saunter with the great King's bluff arm on your neck,
feeling that friend-slaying, terror-dazzled heart
ballooning off into its awful dream –
a noble saying, 'How the King must love you!'
And you, 'If it were a question of my head,
or losing his meanest village in France . . .'
then by the scaffold and the headsman's axe –
'Friend, give me your hand for the first step,
as for coming down, I'll shift for myself.'

Robert Lowell

Thomas More was a scholar, a poet, a philosopher, a Member of Parliament, and a diplomat. He succeeded Wolsey as Lord Chancellor in 1529, but resigned the post in 1532. When Henry VIII failed to obtain a divorce from the Pope, he decided to break with Rome and establish the Church of England, appointing himself as its Supreme Head. Public servants had to take the Oath of Succession which recognized Henry VIII's supremacy over the Pope. More refused to take this Oath and this refusal to compromise his principles led to the scaffold.

1536

THE DEATH OF ANNE BOLEYN

As for them all I do not thus lament,
But as of right my reason doth me bind;
But as the most doth all their deaths repent,
Even so do I by force of mourning mind.
Some say, 'Rochford, haddest thou been not so proud,
For thy great wit each man would thee bemoan,
Since as it is so, many cry aloud
It is great loss that thou art dead and gone.'

Ah! Norris, Norris, my tears begin to run
To think what hap did thee so lead or guide
Whereby thou hast both thee and thine undone
That is bewailed in court of every side;
In place also where thou hast never been
Both man and child doth piteously thee moan.
They say, 'Alas, thou art far overseen
By thine offences to be thus dead and gone.'

Ah! Weston, Weston, that pleasant was and young,
In active things who might with thee compare?

All words accept that thou diddest speak with tongue,
So well esteemed with each where thou diddest fare.

And we that now in court doth lead our life
Most part in mind doth thee lament and moan;
But that thy faults we daily hear so rife,
All we should weep that thou are dead and gone.

Ah! Mark, what moan should I for thee make more,
Since that thy death thou hast deserved best,
Save only that mine eye is forced sore
With piteous plaint to moan thee with the rest?
A time thou haddest above thy poor degree,
The fall whereof thy friends may well bemoan:
A rotten twig upon so high a tree
Hath slipped thy hold, and thou art dead and gone.

And thus farewell each one in hearty wise!
The axe is home, your heads be in the street;
The trickling tears doth fall so from my eyes
I scarce may write, my paper is so wet.
But what can hope when death hath played his part,
Though nature's course will thus lament and moan?
Leave sobs therefore, and every Christian heart
Pray for the souls of those be dead and gone.

attributed to Thomas Wyatt

In 1525 Henry became infatuated with one of the Ladies of the Court, Anne Boleyn, who was ambitious and resolute. Henry showered her with gifts and she went out riding and hunting with him. Around 1531 they started to sleep together and in 1532 she found herself pregnant. Henry, in the meantime, had proclaimed himself the head of the Church in England, and arranged for his divorce from Catherine of Aragon. He married Anne secretly in January 1533; her coronation took lace in June, and in September she gave birth to a daughter, Elizabeth.

Henry, however, wanted a son to secure the stability of his succession. Anne suffered a miscarriage in 1534 and again in 1536. But already the King's eye had alighted on another Lady of the Court, Jane Seymour. At Easter in 1536 Henry and Anne quarrelled in public and Cromwell, Henry's Chief Minister, decided to act. Within four weeks Anne was arrested, tried, executed and buried in the Tower. The charges brought against her included incest with her brother, Rochford, and adultery with the various courtiers named in the poem which is attributed to Thomas Wyatt. Wyatt was also arrested on the grounds that he had been Anne's lover before her marriage, but he was later released.

Cromwell manufactured whatever evidence he needed. Anne may have been flirtatious, but it is unlikely that she was so rash as to have actually deceived Henry. The coup against her worked because she had so many enemies – the friends of Mary Tudor, of the late Thomas More, and of the up-and-coming Seymours. But her greatest enemy was the King himself, who had become bored with her. She was executed on 19 May, and the next day Henry was betrothed to Jane Seymour. Ten days later they were married.

A FINAL WORD FROM HER OWN BOOK OF HOURS

> Remember me when you do pray,
> That hope doth lead from day to day.
> *Anne Boleyn*

1539

THE DISSOLUTION OF THE MONASTERIES

> Little Jack Horner
> Sat in the corner,
> Eating a Christmas pie;
> He put in his thumb,
> And pulled out a plum,
> And said, What a good boy am I!
> *Anonymous*

One interpretation of this otherwise puzzling nursery rhyme is that Jack Horner was steward to the last Abbot of Glastonbury. Hoping to appease Henry VIII's insatiable greed for Church property at a time when the King was presiding over the wholesale dissolution of all monasteries, the Abbot sent Jack to London with a pie in which the title deeds of twelve manors were concealed. On the way Jack opened the pie and extracted the title deed to the manor of Mells. The Horner family did in fact acquire the manor of Mells at the time of the Dissolution, but always claimed that the title was fairly bought.

Opinions on Henry VIII are sharply divided. His defenders argue that he created the Church of England, built up the power of Parliament, made England a force to be reckoned with in European politics, established a strong monarchy, and encouraged the arts. His detractors point out that he pillaged the monasteries to pay off the nobility and his own supporters, and that he was vain, greedy, cruel, lecherous, self-pitying, and treacherous to his friends and ministers. The more one reads about him, indeed, the less attractive does he appear. Dickens was unequivocal: 'The plain truth is, that he was a most intolerable ruffian, a disgrace to human nature, and a blot of blood and grease upon the History of England.'

King Edward VI, 1547–53

1549

Kett's Rebellion

On Mousehold Heath they gathered
Kett's ragtail army, 30,000 peasants.
Below them the city of Norwich
trembled, a mirage in the summer heat.
Mayor Codd and his burgesses
flapping like chickens overcircled by a hawk
sent deputies bowing up the hillside
to bargain for time with bread and meat,
meanwhile sunk their valuables in wells
and out of a secret gate
sped messengers to London squawking for help
against Kett 'that Captain of Mischief'
and his 'parcel of vagabonds . . . brute beasts.'

For six weeks up on Mousehold Heath they sat
high on heather, sky and hope.
' 'Twas a merry world when we were yonder
eating of mutton' one would look back.
The sun poured down like honey

and there was work for work-shaped hands, –
stakes to be sharpened, trenches to be dug,
a New Jerusalem of turf thrown up.
Hacking down the hated fences
and rounding up gentry was for sport.
Meanwhile the Dreamer under the Oak
wrote these words with the tip of his tongue:
'We desire that Bondmen may be free
as Christ made all free, His precious blood shedding.'
The sentries lay back on cupped palms.
Crickets in the dry grass wound their watch.
City-men crawled like ants.
Clouds coasted round the edge . . .

'The country gnoffs, Hob, Dick, and Hick
With clubs and clouted shoon
Shall fill the Vale of Dussindale
With slaughtered bodies soon.'

August 27th, 1549.
A long black cloud against the blood-red sunrise
Warwick and his mounted Landsknechts showed up.
One puff of their cannon
took the skull of Mousehold Heath clean off.
Then down the hill they tumbled
with their pitchforks, their birdslings, their billhooks.
They had no chance, – less
than rabbits making a run for it
when the combine rips into the last patch
and the Guns stand by, about to make laconic remarks.
So they laid themselves down, ripe for sacrifice,
till the brook got tired of undertaking
and Dussindale was bloodily fulfilled.
Kett, found shivering in a barn,
was dragged through the city in ankle-chains
then hung upside down from the castle wall, –
they made fun of Death in those days.

Then Mayor Codd called for a Thanksgiving Mass
followed by feasting in the streets
While many a poor cottage-woman
waiting for her menfolk to come back
heard tapping on the shutters that night
but it was handfuls of rain.

Keith Chandler

During Edward VI's troubled reign there were risings in the West Country against the Reformation, and in Norfolk against enclosure land by capitalist farmers. Kett was a well-off East Anglian tanner; but he put himself at the head of what was in effect a peasants' revolt that posed a major threat to local shire governors. His ragged army captured Norwich. This was the only act of rebellion in the whole of the Tudor period to have social aims – the lowering of rents and the abolition of bond men, game laws and enclosures. The regency government saw it as a serious challenge to the stability of the realm and suppressed it mercilessly, using German mercenaries to kill 3,000 of those involved. A further 300 were hanged. Tudor justice was not tempered by leniency.

Mary Tudor, 1553–1558

1554

ELIZABETH'S IMPRISONMENT

Oh, Fortune! how thy restlesse wavering state
Hath fraught with cares my troubled witt!
Witnes this present prisonn, wither fate
    Could beare me, and the joys I quit.
Thus causedst the guiltie to be losed
From bandes, wherein are innocents inclosed:
    Causing the guiltles to be straite reserved.
    And freeing those that death hath well deserved.
But by her envie can be nothing wroughte,
So God send to my foes all they have thoughte.

Elizabeth I

In 1554 Mary's sister, Elizabeth, was imprisoned after the discovery of a plot to overthrow the Queen, who would also have liked to debar her from succeeding to the throne. Living throughout Mary's reign under the shadow of the scaffold, Elizabeth devoted herself to her studies and was to become one of the most learned of England's monarchs, able to address universities in Latin and ambassadors in their own tongues.

THE PROTESTANT MARTYRS

The Martyrdom of Bishop Farrar

Burned by Bloody Mary's men at Caermarthen. 'If I flinch from
the pain of the burning, believe not the doctrine that I have preached.'
(His words on being chained to the stake.)

Bloody Mary's venomous flames can curl;
They can shrivel sinew and char bone
Of foot, ankle, knee, and thigh, and boil
Bowels, and drop his heart a cinder down;
And her soldiers can cry, as they hurl
Logs in the red rush: 'This is her sermon.'

The sullen-jowled watching Welsh townspeople
Hear him crack in the fire's mouth; they see what
Black oozing twist of stuff bubbles the smell
That tars and retches their lungs: no pulpit
Of his ever held their eyes so still,
Never, as now his agony, his wit.

An ignorant means to establish ownership
Of his flock! Thus their shepherd she seized
And knotted him into this blazing shape
In their eyes, as if such could have cauterized
The trust they turned towards him, and branded on
Its stump her claim, to outlaw question.

So it might have been: seeing their exemplar
And teacher burned for his lessons to black bits,
Their silence might have disowned him to her,
And hung up what he had taught with their Welsh hats:
Who sees his blasphemous father struck by fire
From heaven, might well be heard to speak no oaths.

But the fire that struck here, come from Hell even,
Kindled little heavens in his words
As he fed his body to the flame alive.
Words which, before they will be dumbly spared,
Will burn their body and be tongued with fire
Make paltry folly of flesh and this world's air.

When they saw what annuities of hours
And comfortable blood he burned to get
His words a bare honouring in their ears,
The shrewd townsfolk pocketed them hot:
Stamp was not current but they rang and shone
As good gold as any queen's crown.

Gave all he had, and yet the bargain struck
To a merest farthing his whole agony,
His body's cold-kept miserdom of shrieks
He gave uncounted, while out of his eyes,
Out of his mouth, fire like a glory broke,
And smoke burned his sermons into the skies.

                                        Ted Hughes

Mary was determined to restore England to the Catholic faith, and she got Parliament to revive the medieval heresy laws which would allow Protestants to be rooted out and saved from eternal perdition by being burned in this world rather than the next. In 1555 seventy condemned heretics were burned at the stake, and by the end of Mary's reign the total had exceeded 300. The victims included the bishops Ridley and Latimer, who died in the town ditch at Oxford, and Thomas Cranmer. Such a programme of persecution was politically disastrous, and from it sprang one of the great works of Protestant literature, Foxe's *Book of Martyrs*.

1558

THE DEATH OF MARY TUDOR

Cruel Behold my Heavy Ending

Goodnight is Queen Mary's death:
a lute that bore her heavy end
through city-prisoning towers
and martyrs' candles.

Without her father's desperate gaiety
she clung to confessors
and watched the ghost of a dog
flung through her window at night
ear-clipped
howling the hanging of priests.

Then the lute resolved
the tragic cadence unfulfilled
and the Queen merciful
in all matters but religion
heard the flame of Latimer's cry
and died.

Peter Jones

When, in 1558, France waged war on Spain, the last British possession on the Continent, Calais, was lost. Mary died with the name 'Calais' supposedly engraved on her heart and her subjects celebrated her passing with bonfires in the streets of London.

Queen Elizabeth I, 1558–1603

1583

Sir Humphrey Gilbert

Southward with fleet of ice
   Sailed the corsair Death;
Wild and fast blew the blast,
   And the east-wind was his breath.

His lordly ships of ice
   Glisten in the sun;
On each side, like pennons wide,
   Flashing crystal streamlets run.

His sails of white sea-mist
   Dripped with silver rain;
But where he passed there were cast
   Leaden shadows o'er the main.

Eastward from Campobello
   Sir Humphrey Gilbert sailed;
Three days or more seaward he bore,
   Then, alas! the land-wind failed.

Alas! the land-wind failed,
   And ice-cold grew the night;
And never more, on sea or shore,
   Should Sir Humphrey see the light.

He sat upon the deck,
   The Book was in his hand:
'Do not fear! Heaven is as near,'
   He said, 'by water as by land!'

In the first watch of the night,
   Without a signal's sound,
Out of the sea, mysteriously,
   The fleet of Death rose all around.

The moon and the evening star
  Were hanging in the shrouds;
Every mast, as it passed,
  Seemed to rake the passing clouds.

They grappled with their prize,
  At midnight black and cold!
As of a rock was the shock;
  Heavily the ground-swell rolled.

Southward through day and dark
  They drift in close embrace,
With mist and rain o'er the open main;
  Yet there seems no change of place.

Southward, for ever southward,
  They drift through dark and day;
And like a dream, in the Gulf-stream
  Sinking, vanish all away.
                    Henry Wadsworth Longfellow

Humphrey Gilbert was Sir Walter Ralegh's half-brother, and they journeyed together on voyages of discovery. In 1583 Gilbert established the first British colony in North America at Newfoundland. He published a treatise urging the discovery of the so-called North West Passage to the Indies and he perished looking for it.

1587

THE EXECUTION OF MARY, QUEEN OF SCOTS

Mary, Mary, quite contrary,
How does your garden grow?
With silver bell and cockle shells,
And pretty maids all in a row.
                    Anonymous

The old nursery rhyme is said to be about Mary Stuart. The 'silver bells' are supposed to be used in the Mass, the 'cockle shells' are the badge of St James of Compostela, worn by pilgrims, and the 'pretty maids' are the famous four Marys who attended the Queen of Scots.

Alas! Poor Queen

She was skilled in music and the dance
And the old arts of love
At the court of the poisoned rose
And the perfumed glove,
And gave her beautiful hand
To the pale Dauphin
A triple crown to win –
And she loved little dogs
    And parrots
  And red-legged partridges
And the golden fishes of the Duc de Guise
And a pigeon with a blue ruff
She had from Monsieur d'Elbœuf.

Master John Knox was no friend to her;
She spoke him soft and kind,
Her honeyed words were Satan's lure
The unwary soul to bind.
'Good sir, doth a lissome shape
And a comely face
Offend your God His Grace
Whose Wisdom maketh these
Golden fishes of the Duc de Guise?'

She rode through Liddesdale with a song;
'Ye streams sae wondrous strang,
Oh, mak' me a wrack as I come back
But spare me as I gang.'
While a hill-bird cried and cried
Like a spirit lost
By the grey storm-wind tost.

Consider the way she had to go,
Think of the hungry snare,
The net she herself had woven,
Aware or unaware,
Of the dancing feet grown still,

The blinded eyes –
Queens should be cold and wise,
And she loved little things,
    Parrots
  And red-legged partridges
And the golden fishes of the Duc de Guise
And the pigeon with the blue ruff
She had from Monsieur d'Elbœuf.

Marion Angus

Mary Stuart was in fact Elizabeth's heir, but she was excluded from succession to the English throne by the Act of Supremacy, passed in 1534, because she was a Catholic. Elizabeth saw her as a constant threat none the less. Although kept in virtual imprisonment in England for almost the last twenty years of her life, she continued to inspire plots against the English Queen, and at last, on 1 February 1587, Elizabeth signed her death warrant. Mary was executed on 8 February and her son, James VI of Scotland, who had been brought up by Calvinists, became Elizabeth's heir.

THE PUBLIC EXECUTIONER

Portraits of Tudor Statesmen

Surviving is keeping your eyes open,
Controlling the twitchy apparatus
Of iris, white, cornea, lash and lid.

So the literal painter set it down –
The sharp raptorial look; strained eyeball;
And mail, ruff, bands, beard, anything, to hide
The violently vulnerable neck.

U. A. Fanthorpe

The Public Executioner was one of the busiest public servants in Tudor England. Three Queens were beheaded – Anne Boleyn, Catherine Howard and Mary, Queen of Scots – and one who aspired to be queen, Lady Jane Grey. Other victims were prominent statesmen such as Thomas More and Thomas Cromwell; bishops such as Cranmer, Latimer and Ridley; courtiers such as Surrey and Essex; and many thousands besides.

SIR FRANCIS DRAKE

Drake's Drum

Drake he's in his hammock an' a thousand mile away,
  (Capten, art tha sleepin' there below?),
Slung atween the round shot in Nombre Dios Bay,
  An' dreamin' arl the time o' Plymouth Hoe.
Yarnder lumes the Island, yarnder lie the ships,
  Wi' sailor lads a dancin' heel-an'-toe,
An' the shore-lights flashin', an' the night-tide dashin',
  He sees et arl so plainly as he saw et long ago.

Drake he was a Devon man, an' rüled the Devon seas,
  (Capten, art tha sleepin' there below?),
Rovin' tho' his death fell, he went wi' heart at ease,
  An' dreamin' arl the time o' Plymouth Hoe.
'Take my drum to England, hang et by the shore,
  Strike et when your powder's runnin' low;
If the Dons sight Devon, I'll quit the port o' Heaven,
  An' drum them up the Channel as we drummed them long
    ago.'

Drake he's in his hammock till the great Armadas come,
  (Capten, art tha sleepin' there below?),

Slung atween the round shot, listenin' for the drum,
    An' dreamin' arl the time o' Plymouth Hoe.
Call him on the deep sea, call him up the Sound,
    Call him when ye sail to meet the foe;
Where the old trade's plyin' an' the old flag flyin'
    They shall find him ware an' wakin', as they found him long
        ago!

Henry Newbolt

Elizabethan seamen carried the English flag across the world. Ralegh settled Virginia as a colony of the Crown, Gilbert claimed Newfoundland, John Hawkins shipped slaves from Portuguese West Africa to the Caribbean, and English merchants searching for the North-East Passage to the Indies reached Moscow. In 1572 Francis Drake delivered a severe blow to Spain, England's major rival in foreign trade and colonial expansion, when at Nombre de Dios on the Panama isthmus he intercepted the Spanish mule convoy bearing silver from Peru. From 1577 to 1580 he sailed his ship, *The Golden Hind*, around the world and was knighted by the Queen on his return. Elizabeth was not only proud of her merchant adventurers, but also a shareholder in several of their expeditions. In 1587 Drake made a daring pre-emptive strike against the Spanish fleet where it lay in the harbour of Cadiz, and in 1588 he helped destroy the Armada as it sailed to invade England.

The Looking-Glass

(*A Country Dance*)

Queen Bess was Harry's daughter. Stand forward partners all!
    In ruff and stomacher and gown
She danced King Philip down-a-down,
And left her shoe to show 'twas true –
    (*The very tune I'm playing you*)
In Norgem at Brickwall!

The Queen was in her chamber, and she was middling old.
Her petticoat was satin, and her stomacher was gold.
Backwards and forwards and sideways did she pass,
Making up her mind to face the cruel looking-glass.
The cruel looking-glass that will never show a lass
As comely or as kindly or as young as what she was!

Queen Bess was Harry's daughter. Now hand your partners all!

The Queen was in her chamber, a-combing of her hair.
There came Queen Mary's spirit and It stood behind her chair,
Singing 'Backwards and forwards and sideways may you pass,
But I will stand behind you till you face the looking-glass.
The cruel looking-glass that will never show a lass
As lovely or unlucky or as lonely as I was!'

Queen Bess was Harry's daughter. Now turn your partners all!

The Queen was in her chamber, a-weeping very sore,
There came Lord Leicester's spirit and It scratched upon the
    door,
Singing 'Backwards and forwards and sideways may you pass,
But I will walk beside you till you face the looking-glass.
The cruel looking-glass that will never show a lass,
As hard and unforgiving or as wicked as you was!'

Queen Bess was Harry's daughter. Now kiss your partners all!

The Queen was in her chamber, her sins were on her head.
She looked the spirits up and down and statelily she said: –
'Backwards and forwards and sideways though I've been,
Yet I am Harry's daughter and I am England's Queen!'
And she faces the looking-glass (and whatever else there was)
And she saw her day was over and she saw her beauty pass
In the cruel looking-glass, that can always hurt a lass
More hard than any ghost there is or any man there was!

                                    Rudyard Kipling

1603

THE DEATH OF ELIZABETH I

Gloriana Dying

None shall gainsay me. I will lie on the floor.
Hitherto from horseback, throne, balcony,
I have looked down upon your looking up.
Those sands are run. Now I reverse the glass
And bid henceforth your homage downward, falling
Obedient and unheeded as leaves in autumn
To quilt the wakeful study I must make
Examining my kingdom from below.
How tall my people are! Like a race of trees
They sway, sigh, nod heads, rustle above me,
And their attentive eyes are distant as starshine.
I have still cherished the handsome and well-made:
No queen has better masts within her forests
Growing, nor prouder and more restive minds
Scabbarded in the loyalty of subjects;
No virgin has had better worship than I.
No, no! Leave me alone, woman! I will not
Be put into a bed. Do you suppose
That I who've ridden through all weathers, danced
Under a treasury's weight of jewels, sat
Myself to stone through sermons and addresses,
Shall come to harm by sleeping on a floor?
Not that I sleep. A bed were good enough
If that were in my mind. But I am here
For a deep study and contemplation,
And as Persephone, and the red vixen,
Go underground to sharpen their wits,
I have left my dais to learn a new policy
Through watching of your feet, and as the Indian
Lays all his listening body along the earth
I lie in wait for the reverberation
Of things to come and dangers threatening.
Is that the Bishop praying? Let him pray on.

If his knees tire his faith can cushion them.
How the poor man grieves Heaven with news of me!
Deposuit superbos. But no hand
Other than my own has put me down –
Not feebleness enforced on brain or limb,
Not fear, misgiving, fantasy, age, palsy,
Has felled me. I lie here by my own will,
And by the curiosity of a queen.
I dare say there is not in all England
One who lies closer to the ground than I.
Not the traitor in the condemned hold
Whose few straws edge away from under his weight
Of ironed fatality; not the shepherd
Huddled for cold under the hawthorn bush,
Nor the long dreaming country lad who lies
Scorching his book before the dying brand.

Sylvia Townsend Warner

Elizabeth died at Richmond Palace on 24 March 1603. She had reached the great age of seventy. A horseman waiting below her room was thrown one of the rings she had been wearing, and with this proof of her death galloped off to Scotland where James VI was expecting it. In the library at Chequers there is a ring in the shape of a skull which is said to be that ring.

The Stuarts, 1603–1715

In the seventeenth century there was a great constitutional conflict which ended with Parliament establishing its supremacy over the monarchy. James I and Charles I believed in the Divine Right of Kings which, in practice, meant that the king and his personal advisers ruled the country.

Both James I and Charles I tried to rule without Parliament, using various devices to raise money, but in 1640 Charles was forced to summon Parliament. When the merchants, country landowners, important farmers and squires, who made up Parliament, met together, they decided to assert their authority, which led to the Civil War from 1642–45.

Oliver Cromwell, an East Anglian country gentleman and farmer, became the leader of the Parliamentary forces. He tried to retain the monarchy in a more limited form, but when the debates with the King led to no satisfactory solution Charles was tried and executed. Cromwell established the Protectorate, which did not even survive his own death. In 1660, Charles I's son was restored to the throne as Charles II.

He too tried to govern without the surveillance of Parliament. His brother, James, who succeeded him in 1685, went one step further and attempted to restore Catholicism in Britain. This was too much for many of the leading families in the land who united to eject James from the throne. This was the Glorious Revolution of 1688 and the Bill of Rights passed by Parliament stated that only a Protestant should succeed to the English Crown. That Bill also brought the King's power under the sanction of Parliament and it forms the basis of today's Parliamentary system.

As James I was also James VI of the Scotland, the two Crowns of England and Scotland were united from 1603, but the two countries were not united until 1707.

The seventeenth century was one of the most creative periods in Britain's history: in literature there were Shakespeare, Milton and Dryden; in music, Purcell; in architecture, Christopher Wren; in science, Isaac Newton.

King James I, 1603–25

James I

The child of Mary Queen of Scots,
    A shifty mother's shiftless son,
Bred up among intrigues and plots,
    Learnèd in all things, wise in none.
Ungainly, babbling, wasteful, weak,
    Shrewd, clever, cowardly, pedantic,
The sights of steel would blanch his cheek,
    The smell of baccy drive him frantic,
He was the author of his line –
    He wrote that witches should be burnt;
He wrote that monarchs were divine,
    And left a son who – proved they weren't!
                    Rudyard Kipling

James VI of Scotland was crowned James I of England. The two most enduring achievements of his reign were literary: the publication in 1611 of the King James Version of the English Bible, on which a committee had been working since 1604, and in 1623 of the First Folio of Shakespeare's plays. Both served to enlarge, enrich and enshrine the great glory of the English language. Early settlers in Jamestown, Virginia, and in New England had as their resource a language that was to become the mother tongue of a mighty continent.

1605

Gunpowder Plot Day

Remember, remember
The fifth of November,
The Gunpowder Treason and Plot;
I see no reason why gunpowder treason
Should ever be forgot.
A stick and a stake
For George's sake

So please remember the bonfire.
Fifty barrels lay below
To blow old England's overthrow.
With a dark lantern and a lighted match
That's the way old Guy was catch.
  Holler, boys, holler; make the bells ring!
  Holler, boys, holler; God save the King!
Anonymous

The Gunpowder Plotters were disappointed that James, whose wife had secretly turned Catholic, had not relaxed the laws against Catholics in general. They plotted to do away with King and Parliament, but they were betrayed by Francis Tresham, who could not bear the thought of his own kinsmen being blown to eternity by the barrels of gunpowder which Guido Fawkes was to ignite. After the plot had been discovered, Catholics were debarred from all public office and forbidden to venture more than five miles from their homes.

1605

ENGLISH SETTLEMENTS IN AMERICA

from **To the Virginian Voyage**

You brave heroic minds,
Worthy your country's name,
That honour still pursue,
Go and subdue;
Whilst loitering hinds
Lurk here at home with shame.

Britons, you stay too long;
Quickly aboard bestow you,
And with a merry gale
Swell your stretched sail,
With vows as strong,
As the winds that blow you.

Your course securely steer;
West and by South forth keep:
Rocks, lee shores, nor shoals,
When Eolus scolds,
You need not fear,
So absolute the deep.

And cheerfully at sea
Success you still entice
To get the pearl and gold;
And ours to hold
Virginia.
Earth's only paradise.

Where nature has in store
Fowl, venison and fish;
And the fruitfullest soil,
Without your toil,
Three harvests more,
All greater than your wish.

> And in regions far
> Such heroes bring you forth,
>   As those from whom we came;
>   And plant our name
> Under the star
> Not known unto our North.
>   *Michael Drayton*

In 1603, England had no colonies, but by 1660 she had the beginnings of an empire. In James's reign the flag was raised in India, the East Indies, Virginia and Massachusetts. In 1601, pioneers landed at Chesapeake Bay, sailed up what was to be called the James River and landed at the site of Jamestown. Their early years proved a struggle and their numbers were soon reduced from 142 to 38; but in 1617 they sent back to England what was to be the source of their subsequent wealth – a cargo of Virginia tobacco.

The first colonists were people who sought adventure, land, wealth and religious freedom. In 1620 a band of Puritans, the 'Pilgrim Fathers', sailed from Plymouth in the *Mayflower* to found a new plantation which, after twenty years, amounted to some 600 people. James I did little to help this colonial expansion, his only gesture being to order the exportation of criminals to Virginia. Charles I did scarcely better. It was left to Oliver Cromwell to be the first real imperialist, when he recognized the necessity for an efficient organization of sea power that would enable England to defend its colonies and attack the colonies of others.

1616

THE DEATH OF SHAKESPEARE

To the Memory of my Beloved Mr William Shakespeare

> I, therefore, will begin. Soul of the Age!
>   The applause, delight, the wonder of our Stage!
> My Shakespeare, rise; I will not lodge thee by
>   Chaucer, or Spenser, or bid Beaumont lie
> A little further, to make thee a room:
>   Thou art a monument, without a tomb,
> And art alive still, while thy book doth live,

And we have wits to read and praise to give.
That I not mix thee so, my brain excuses;
  I mean with great, but disproportioned Muses:
For, if I thought my judgement were of years,
  I should commit thee surely with thy peers,
And tell how far thou didst our Lyly out-shine,
  Or sporting Kyd, or Marlowe's mighty line.
And though thou hadst small Latin and less Greek,
  From thence to honour thee, I would not seek
For names; but call forth thundering Æschylus,
  Euripides, and Sophocles to us,
Paccuvius, Accius, him of Cordova dead,
  To life again, to hear thy buskin tread,
And shake a stage; or, when thy socks were on,
  Leave thee alone, for the comparison
Of all that insolent Greece or haughty Rome
  Sent forth, or since did from their ashes come.
Triumph, my Britain, thou hast one to show
  To whom all scenes of Europe homage owe.
He was not of an age but for all time!
  And all the Muses still were in their prime
When, like Apollo, he came forth to warm
  Our ears, or, like a Mercury, to charm!

Ben Jonson

1618

THE EXECUTION OF SIR WALTER RALEGH

His Epitaph

Which He Writ the Night Before His Execution

Even such is time, that takes in trust
  Our youth, our joys, our all we have,
And pays us but with age and dust;
  Who in the dark and silent grave,
When we have wandered all our ways,

Shuts up the story of our days!
But from this earth, this grave, this dust,
The Lord shall raise me up, I trust!
                                    Walter Ralegh

Ralegh had been condemned to death in 1603 on trumped-up charges.
Reprieved, he lived in the Tower of London until 1616, when he was
released and put in charge of a disastrous expedition to find Eldorado.
Spiteful and petty as ever, James I took it upon himself to strike down
the last of the Elizabethans, who by then was nearly seventy years old.
When, at the second stroke of the axe, Ralegh's head fell from his body,
a voice from the crowd in the New Palace Yard cried out, 'We have not
such another head to be cut off.'

King Charles I, 1625–49

THE THREAT TO THE KING

from The Secret People

The face of the King's servants grew greater than the King.
He tricked them and they trapped him and drew round him
    in a ring;
The new grave lords closed round him that had eaten the
    abbey's fruits,
And the men of the new religion with their Bibles in their boots,
We saw their shoulders moving to menace and discuss.
And some were pure and some were vile, but none took heed
    of us;
We saw the King when they killed him, and his face was proud
    and pale,
And a few men talked of freedom while England talked of ale.

G. K. Chesterton

James I had believed in the theory of the Divine Right of Kings, and his son Charles tried to implement it in the 1630s. The question was whether the King could rule without Parliament. The Members of Parliament themselves, moneyed and landed men, asserted their representative rights against royal absolutism. The principles for which they stood were a far cry from democracy and general suffrage, but those ideals have their beginning in this conflict, and the Civil War to which it eventually led probably prevented revolution at a later date. Colonel Thomas Rainborough, MP for Droitwich, pointed the way forward when he said: 'I think the meanest He that is in England hath a life as well as the greatest He; and therefore, truly sir, I think that every man that is to live under a government ought, first, by his own consent to put himself under that government.'

1642

THE BATTLE OF EDGEHILL

After Edgehill, 1642

1 Villagers Report 'The Late Apparitions'

A December Saturday, star-clear
at Kineton. Three months since the battle,
the village collects itself – Christmas
perhaps a demarcation, a control
in the blood-letting. Yet on the ridge
of Edge Hill, the night resounds,
armies grinding one against the other
re-enacting the action, re-dying the deaths.

Shepherds hear trumpets, drums –
expect a visitation of holy kings with retinues.
Instead, the spectral soldiers strike,
icy night skies crack with cries,
steel clashing and the sput of muskets.
A knot of Kineton men watch, witness;
Samuel Marshall, the Minister, says
the Devil's apparitions seize the dead.

2 A Ghost Speaks

I am unplanted, my world this waste –
the heath where bone was split, undressed of flesh,
where arteries unleashed their flood, the colour
of death. What is the colour of honour? The blue
in which we dissolve into air? the white of ashes?
Can I be woven into the braids of her hair, my lady,
or exist in the quick of my son's fingernails?
I, who carried the Standard, once drove the plough,
turning up earth, the harvest of worms. Now I envy
the seeds in the furrow, their dark cradle.

My blood is this Midlands field, this hacked hedgerow
where I lie, hearing the drumbeat of the dead,

corpses strewn rotting, graveless.
I glide up and down these rows of human manure,
the faces of soldiers like fallen cameos.
Here is Sir Edmund Verney, Thomas Transome –
they look skywards, lolling near my own wistful face.
Sir Edmund is grimacing slightly as he did in life,
Thomas Transome's skull a broken eggshell.

The brittle linnet flies from me. Dry leaves relinquish
their hold on twigs. A hare sits motionless, watching,
listening to last groans forever in the wind.

I see a troop of Horse on the skyline – Parliament's.
They charge our pikemen; now they vanish
like moving cloud-shadows across the field.
I cannot follow the clouds; I am chained to my carcass
hovering, as others are, above their unburied selves.

3 A Dragoon Observes Colonel Cromwell

Like a falcon from the gauntlet, he throws off these deaths.
He tells us 'Smile out to God in Praise', for his is the sword
of the Lord. I see his horse, piebald with blood.

                                                    Gladys Mary Coles

In August 1642 Charles raised his standard at Nottingham and the first battle of the Civil War took place at Edgehill on 23 October. Charles's German nephew, Prince Rupert, led one of his famous cavalry charges, which swept everything before it, but ran out of control. The foot-soldiers of the Parliamentary army held on doggedly. The Royalist Sir Edmund Verney was killed clutching the standard so firmly that his right hand had to be cut off. William Harvey, the scientist, who also fought, pulled a dead body over himself as he lay wounded, to protect himself against the freezing cold. Oliver Cromwell did not take part in this battle, for it seems that he arrived too late, but he took notice of what had happened and resolved to reorganize his army accordingly. Strange rumours soon began to circulate about Edgehill: shepherds claimed to have heard unaccountable sounds of battle – shots, trumpets and drums – while ghostly soldiers were seen riding and fighting. Charles sent agents to investigate these reports and pamphlets were written by both sides alleging that divine messages could be read in them.

1643

To Lucasta, Going to the Wars

Tell me not, Sweet, I am unkind,
    That from the nunnery
Of thy chaste breast and quiet mind
    To war and arms I fly.

True, a new mistress now I chase,
    The first foe in the field;
And with a stronger faith embrace
    A sword, a horse, a shield.

Yet this inconstancy is such
    As thou too shalt adore;
I could not love thee, Dear, so much,
    Loved I not Honour more.

Richard Lovelace

1645

The Battle of Naseby

Oh! wherefore come ye forth, in triumph from the North,
    With your hands, and your feet, and your raiment all red?
And wherefore doth your rout sent forth a joyous shout?
    And whence be the grapes of the wine-press which ye tread?

Oh evil was the root, and bitter was the fruit,
    And crimson was the juice of the vintage that we trod;
For we trampled on the throng of the haughty and the strong,
    Who sate in the high places, and slew the saints of God.

It was about the noon of a glorious day in June,
    That we saw their banners dance, and their cuirasses shine,
And the Man of Blood was there, with his long essenced hair,
    And Astley, and Sir Marmaduke, and Rupert of the Rhine.

Like a servant of the Lord, with his Bible and his sword,
　　The General rode along us to form us to the fight,
When a murmuring sound broke out, and swell'd into a shout,
　　Among the godless horsemen upon the tyrant's right.

And hark! like the roar of the billows on the shore,
　　The cry of battle rises along their charging line!
For God! for the Cause! for the Church, for the Laws!
　　For Charles King of England, and Rupert of the Rhine!

The furious German comes, with his clarions and his drums,
　　His bravoes of Alsatia, and pages of Whitehall;
They are bursting on our flanks. Grasp your pikes, close your
　　ranks;
　　For Rupert never comes but to conquer or to fall.

They are here! They rush on! We are broken! We are gone!
　　Our left is borne before them like stubble on the blast.
O Lord, put forth thy might! O Lord, defend the right!
　　Stand back to back, in God's name, and fight it to the last.

Stout Skippon hath a wound; the centre hath given ground:
　　Hark! hark! – What means the trampling of horsemen on our
　　rear?
Whose banner do I see, boys? 'Tis he, thank God! 'tis he, boys,
　　Bear up another minute: brave Oliver is here.

Their heads all stooping low, their points all in a row,
　　Like a whirlwind on the trees, like a deluge on the dikes,
Our cuirassiers have burst on the ranks of the accurst,
　　And at a shock have scattered the forest of his pikes.

Fast, fast, the gallants ride, in some safe nook to hide
　　Their coward heads, predestined to rot on Temple Bar:
And he – he turns, he flies: – shame on those cruel eyes
　　That bore to look on torture, and dare not look on war.

Ho! comrades, scour the plain; and, ere ye strip the slain,
　　First give another stab to make your search secure,
Then shake from sleeves and pockets their broadpieces and
　　lockets,
　　The tokens of the wanton, the plunder of the poor.

Fools, your doublets shone with gold, and your hearts were gay
    and bold,
    When you kissed your lily hands to your lemans today;
And tomorrow shall the fox, from her chambers in the rocks,
    Lead forth her tawny cubs to howl above the prey.

Where be your tongues that late mocked at heaven and hell and
    fate,
    And the fingers that once were so busy with your blades,
Your perfumed satin clothes, your catches and your oaths,
    Your stage-plays and your sonnets, your diamonds and your
    spades?

Down, down, for ever down with the mitre and the crown,
    With the Belial of the Court, and the Mammon of the Pope;
There is woe in Oxford Halls; there is wail in Durham's Stalls:
    The Jesuit smites his bosom; the Bishop rends his cope.

And She of the seven hills shall mourn her children's ills,
    And tremble when she thinks of the edge of England's sword;
And the Kings of earth in fear shall shudder when they hear.
    What the hand of God hath wrought for the Houses and the
    Word.

Thomas Babington, Lord Macaulay

This splendid poem describes the decisive battle of the Civil War. The
Royalist troops were heavily outnumbered by Roundheads, largely
because the forces led by Lord Goring, who was jealous of Prince
Rupert, failed to turn up. A brilliant charge by Rupert nearly won the
day, but Cromwell's cavalry stood firm. Macaulay, in his enthusiasm
for the Protestant and Parliamentary cause, overlooked the fact that
Cromwell's men brutally murdered as many of the Royalist women
camp-followers as they could lay their hands on. As usual, Cromwell
had no doubts about the reason for his victory: 'Sir, there is none other
than the hand of God.'

1649

THE EXECUTION OF CHARLES I

from **An Horatian Ode upon Cromwell's Return from Ireland**

What field of all the civil wars
Where his were not the deepest scars?
  And Hampton shows what part
  He had of wiser art;

Where, twining subtle fears with hope,
He wove a net of such a scope
  That Charles himself might chase
  To Car'sbrook's narrow case;

That thence the Royal Actor borne
The tragic scaffold might adorn:
  While round the armèd bands
  Did clap their bloody hands.

He nothing common did or mean
Upon that memorable scene,
  But with his keener eye
  The axe's edge did try;

Nor called the Gods, with vulgar spite,
To vindicate his helpless right;
   But bowed his comely head
   Down, as upon a bed.

This was that memorable hour
Which first assured the forcèd power:
   So when they did design
   The Capitol's first line,

A bleeding head, where they begun,
Did fright the architects to run;
   And yet in that the State
   Foresaw its happy fate!

Andrew Marvell

This is an extract from a poem written to celebrate Cromwell's triumphant return from Ireland in 1650. Marvell recognizes Charles's courage and serenity, but has no doubts about the justice of the Parliamentarian cause.

The Commonwealth, 1649–60

OLIVER CROMWELL, 1649–1658

> Rupert of the Rhine
> Thought Cromwell was a swine.
> He felt quite sure
> After Marston Moor
>
> *E. C. Bentley*

To the Lord General Cromwell

Cromwell, our chief of men, who through a cloud
   Not of war only, but detractions rude,
   Guided by faith and matchless fortitude,
   To peace and truth thy glorious way hast ploughed,
And on the neck of crownèd Fortune proud
   Hast reared God's trophies, and his work pursued;
   While Darwen stream, with blood of Scots imbrued,
   And Dunbar field resounds thy praises loud,
And Worcester's laureate wreath: yet much remains
   To conquer still; Peace hath her victories
   No less renowned than War: new foes arise,
Threatening to bind our souls with secular chains.
   Help us to save free conscience from the paw
   Of hireling wolves, whose Gospel is their maw.

          John Milton

Cromwell, a wealthy East Anglian farmer, became an MP in the Long Parliament, but emerged after the Roundhead victories in 1644 and 1645 as the leader of the Protestant revolution. He routed the Royalists in the second civil war of 1648, and then came to accept that Charles must be executed. He ruthlessly crushed the uprisings that took place after Charles's death: in Ireland in 1650; among the Scots in the same year; and in England in 1651 – this last ending with his victory at Worcester. In 1653 he became Lord Protector and, even more quickly than Charles, fell out with Parliament, crying: 'Take away that fool's bauble, the mace!' Thereafter he ruled England not with MPs, but with Major-Generals. His devotion to the cause of parliamentary democracy is recognized by the statue of him erected outside the public entrance to the House of Commons.

1649

from The Diggers' Song

You noble Diggers all, stand up now, stand up now,
  You noble Diggers all, stand up now,
The waste land to maintain, seeing Cavaliers by name
Your digging do disdain and persons all defame.
    Stand up now, stand up now.

Your houses they pull down, stand up now, stand up now,
  Your houses they pull down, stand up now;
Your houses they pull down to fright poor men in town,
But the Gentry must come down, and the poor shall wear
  the crown.
    Stand up now, Diggers all!

The Lawyers they conjoin, stand up now, stand up now,
  The Lawyers they conjoin, stand up now!
To arrest you they advise, such fury they devise,
The devil in them lies, and hath blinded both their eyes.
    Stand up now, stand up now.

The Clergy they come in, stand up now, stand up now,
  The Clergy they come in, stand up now;
The Clergy they come in, and say it is a sin
That we should now begin our freedom for to win.
    Stand up now, Diggers all!

The Cavaliers are foes, stand up now, stand up now,
  The Cavaliers are foes, stand up now;
The Cavaliers are foes, themselves they do disclose
By verses, not in prose, to please the singing boys.
    Stand up now, Diggers all!

To conquer them by love, come in now, come in now,
  To conquer them by love, come in now;
To conquer them by love, as it does you behove,
For He is King above, no Power is like to Love.
    Glory here, Diggers all!

                                        Gerrard Winstanley

A ferment of revolutionary ideas was released during the 1640s. The Levellers, led by John Lilburne, advocated equality for all, but a weaver from Wigan, Gerrard Winstanley, went further. He demanded the communal ownership of all property. In 1649, with a band of twenty followers, he occupied some common land on St George's Hill in Surrey, his stated purpose being 'to sow corn for the succour of men'. Cromwell would not have any of this, and the Diggers were moved on and dispersed a year later.

1658

THE DEATH OF CROMWELL

from **A Poem upon the Death of His late Highnesse the Lord Protector**

I saw him dead, a leaden slumber lyes
And mortall sleep over those wakefull eys:
Those gentle Rayes under the lidds were fled
Which through his lookes that piercing sweetnesse shed:
That port which so Majestique was and strong,
Loose and depriv'd of vigour stretch'd along:
All wither'd, all discolour'd, pale and wan,
How much another thing, no more that man?
Oh human glory vaine, Oh death, Oh wings,
Oh worthless world, Oh transitory things!

Thee many ages hence in martiall verse
Shall th' English souldier ere he charge rehearse:
Singing of thee inflame themselvs to fight
And with the name of Cromwell armyes fright.
As long as rivers to the seas shall runne,
As long as Cynthia shall relieve the sunne,
While staggs shall fly unto the forests thick,
While sheep delight the grassy downs to pick,
As long as future time succeeds the past,
Always thy honour, praise and name shall last.

Andrew Marvell

Cromwell suffered from malaria, called marsh-fever in his day. During the 1630s the wife of a Spanish envoy in Lima, who had been cured of malaria by the use of quinine, popularized it in Europe. Quinine is a powder made from the bark of a tree, the Cinchona, named after her. It also came to be known as 'Jesuit's Bark'. Cromwell could have taken it and been cured, but he died, as he had lived, a Protestant bigot, calling quinine 'the powder of the Devil'.

King Charles II, 1660–85

We have a pritty witty king
  And whose word no man relys on:
He never said a foolish thing,
  And never did a wise one.
    John Wilmot, Earl of Rochester

In 1660 the Puritan Revolution petered out. So another experiment was tried – the restoration of the monarchy. Charles I's son returned from exile and became Charles II. Those who had signed the death warrant of the previous King were mercilessly pursued and Cromwell's body was dug up, hung in chains and his skull exhibited on a pike. The Book of Common Prayer was reintroduced, and the Test Acts were passed to keep Dissenters and Catholics alike out of office.

Parliament struggled to reassert its power and denied the supply of money to the King. Charles circumvented this by taking large bribes from Louis XIV of France. England fought Holland and allied herself with France, though many people would have preferred the opposite. The political situation was dominated by Charles's inability to produce an heir, although this was not for want of trying.

Some historians have praised the Puritan Revolution, while condemning the profligacy, deceitfulness and self-indulgence of the court of Charles II. Yet this was also an age which produced England's greatest scientist, Newton, its greatest architect, Wren, and its greatest political poet, John Dryden.

1665

THE GREAT PLAGUE

Ring-a-ring o' roses,
A pocket full of posies,
  A-tishoo! A-tishoo!
We all fall down
  Anonymous

This nursery rhyme is said to date from the time of the Great Plague itself. The give-away symptom was a rash of red spots, and people tried to fend off the infection by carrying nosegays of herbs. As the sickness

developed, breathing became more difficult before the inevitability of
death.

1666

THE GREAT FIRE OF LONDON

from **Annus Mirabilis**

The fire, mean time, walks in a broader gross,
  To either hand his wings he opens wide:
He wades the streets, and straight he reaches cross,
  And plays his longing flames on th' other side.

At first they warm, then scorch, and then they take:
  Now with long necks from side to side they feed:
At length, grown strong, their Mother fire forsake,
  And a new Collony of flames succeed.

To every nobler portion of the Town,
  The curling billows roul their restless Tyde:
In parties now they straggle up and down,
  As Armies, unoppos'd, for prey divide.

One mighty Squadron, with a side wind sped,
  Through narrow lanes his cumber'd fire does haste:
By pow'rful charms of gold and silver led,
  The *Lombard* Banquers and the *Change* to waste.

Another backward to the *Tow'r* would go,
  And slowly eats his way against the wind:
But the main body of the marching foe
  Against th' Imperial Palace is design'd.

Now day appears, and with the day the King,
  Whose early care had robb'd him of his rest:
Far off the cracks of falling houses ring,
  And shrieks of subjects pierce his tender breast.

Near as he draws, thick harbingers of smoke,
  With gloomy pillars, cover all the place:

Whose little intervals of night are broke
    By sparks that drive against his Sacred Face.

Nor with an idle care did he behold:
    (Subjects may grieve, but Monarchs must redress.)
He chears the fearful, and commends the bold,
    And makes despairers hope for good success.

Himself directs what first is to be done,
    And orders all the succours which they bring.
The helpful and the good about him run,
    And form an Army worthy such a King.

He sees the dire contagion spread so fast,
    That where it seizes, all relief is vain:
And therefore must unwillingly lay waste
    That Country which would, else, the foe maintain.

The powder blows up all before the fire:
    Th' amazed flames stand gather'd on a heap;
And from the precipices brinck retire,
    Afraid to venture on so large a leap.

Thus fighting fires a while themselves consume,
    But straight, like *Turks*, forc'd on to win or die,
They first lay tender bridges of their fume,
    And o'r the breach in unctuous vapours flie.

Part stays for passage till a gust of wind
   Ships o'r their forces in a shining sheet:
Part, creeping under ground, their journey blind,
   And, climbing from below, their fellows meet.

Thus, to some desart plain, or old wood side,
   Dire night-hags come from far to dance their round:
And o'r brode Rivers on their fiends they ride,
   Or sweep in clowds above the blasted ground.

No help avails: for, *Hydra*-like, the fire,
   Lifts up his hundred heads to aim his way.
And scarce the wealthy can one half retire,
   Before he rushes in to share the prey.

                        John Dryden

The Great Plague had carried off as many as 68,000 Londoners and in the following year the Great Fire destroyed the heart of the city. Yet this provided the opportunity for the architects of the time, most notably Sir Christopher Wren, to redesign London in a more planned way and to erect some of the most beautiful buildings since the medieval cathedrals. Wren's epitaph, composed by his son, is inscribed over the north door inside St Paul's Cathedral and reads: 'Si monumentum requiris, circumspice' ('If you seek his monument, look around').

1671

THE ATTEMPT ON THE CROWN JEWELS

On Blood's Stealing the Crown

When daring Blood, his rents to have regain'd
Upon the English diadem distrain'd,
He chose the cassock, surcingle, and gown
(No mask so fit for one that robs a crown),
But his lay-pity underneath prevail'd,
And while he spar'd the Keeper's life, he fail'd.
With the priest's vestments had he but put on
A bishop's cruelty, the crown was gone.

                        Andrew Marvell

Colonel Blood, an adventurer seeking redress over a land dispute, made an ingenious plan to steal the Crown Jewels. Under the disguise of a priest, he ingratiated himself with the Keeper of the Jewel House, Talbot Edwards, and was granted a special viewing, whereupon he and his companions turned upon Edwards and bound and gagged him. One stuffed the Orb down his breeches, another tried to saw the Sceptre in half, and Blood popped the Crown under his priest's cloak. Unfortunately for them, at that very moment Edwards's son returned on leave from Flanders and they were captured. Charles II pardoned Blood, possibly because he had proven himself too valuable as a spy.

1681

THE EARL OF SHAFTESBURY

from **Absalom and Achitophel**

Of these the false Achitophel was first,
A name to all succeeding ages curst.
For close designs and crooked counsels fit;
Sagacious, bold, and turbulent of wit.
Restless, unfix'd in principles and place;
In pow'r unpleas'd, impatient of disgrace.
A fiery soul which, working out its way,
Fretted the pigmy body to decay,
And o'er-inform'd the tenement of clay.
A daring pilot in extremity;
Pleas'd with the danger, when the waves went high
He sought the storms; but, for a calm unfit,
Would steer too nigh the sands to boast his wit.
Great wits are sure to madness near alli'd,
And thin partitions do their bounds divide;
Else why should he, with wealth and honor blest,
Refuse his age the needful hours of rest?
Punish a body which he could not please;
Bankrupt of life, yet prodigal of ease?

John Dryden

'Absalom and Achitophel' is perhaps the finest political poem in the English language. Asked to write it by the King, Dryden applied his majestic Augustan couplets to satirizing the political party known as the Whigs, and particularly, in the figure of Achitophel, Anthony Ashley Cooper, the Earl of Shaftesbury, who had been arrested for high treason in July 1681. Shaftesbury had led the Whig opposition to the King, openly supporting the Duke of Monmouth as Protestant heir to the throne; masterminding the campaign to exclude the King's brother, James; and striving to ensure that Parliament was not suspended. He had, in effect, created the post of Leader of the Opposition.

King James II, 1685–8

from The Statue in Stocks-Market

But with all his faults restore us our King,
If ever you hope in December for Spring;
For though all the world cannot show such another,
Yet we'd rather have him than his bigoted brother.

Andrew Marvell

James II set out to restore Catholicism to England at breakneck speed. Within ten days of his accession, he attended a Mass in public. The Test Acts, excluding all Dissenters from state office, were his main stumbling-block, and so he revived the power to dispense with inconvenient laws, just as his father, Charles I, had tried to do. He suspended Parliament and strengthened the standing army. When seven Protestant bishops refused to read one of his declarations from the pulpit, he had them arrested and put on trial. Although they were acquitted, this gesture did more than anything to turn opinion against the King. But the last straw was the birth of a son as Prince of Wales in June 1688, which in effect barred James's two Protestant daughters – Mary, married to William of Orange, and Anne, married to Prince George of Denmark – from the throne. William, however, had been making his own preparations, egged on by Protestant exiles, and in 1688 the people of England appealed to him to release them from 'Popery and slavery'.

1685

MONMOUTH'S REBELLION

Monmouth Degraded

(*Or, James Scott, the Little King in Lyme*)

Come beat alarm, sound a charge
As well without as in the verge,
Let every sword and soul be large
  To make our monarch shine, boys.

Let's leave off whores and drunken souls
And windy words o'er brimming bowls,
Let English hearts exceed the Poles'
    'Gainst Perkin, King in Lyme, boys.

Such a fop-king was ne'er before
Is landed on our western shore,
Which our black saints do all adore,
Inspir'd by Tub-Divine, boys.
Let us assume the souls of Mars
And march in order, foot and horse,
Pull down the standard at the cross
    Of Perkin, King in Lyme, boys.

Pretended son unto a King,
Subject of delights in sin,
The most ungrateful wretch of men;
    Dishonour to the shrine, boys
Of Charles, and James the undoubted right
Of England's crown and honours bright:
While he can find us work, let's fight
    'Gainst Perkin, King in Lyme, boys.

The Sainted Sisters now look blue,
Their cant's all false if God be true;
Their teaching stallions dare not do
    No more but squeeze and whine, boys;
Exhorting all the clowns to fight
Against their God, King, Church, and Right,
Takes care, for all their wives at night,
    For Perkin, King in Lyme, boys.

'Poor Perkin' now he is no more,
But James Scott as he was before;
No honour left but soul to soar
    Till quite expir'd with time, boys.
But first he'll call his parliament
By Ferguson and Grey's consent,
Trenchard and all the boors in's tent,
    Fit for the King in Lyme, boys.

'Gainst these mock kings, each draw his sword;
In blood we'll print them on record,
'Traitors against their sovereign lord';
    Let's always fight and join, boys.
Now they're block'd up by sea and land,
By treason they must fall or stand,
We only wait the King's command
    To burn the rogues in Lyme, boys.

But now we hear they're salli'd forth,
Front and flank 'em, south and north,
Nobles of brave England's worth,
    Let your bright honours shine, boys.
Let guns and cannons roar and ring
The music of a warlike King,
And all the gods just conquest bring
    Against the rogues in Lyme, boys.
                                    Anonymous

The handsome bastard son of Charles II, the Duke of Monmouth, left
his mistress in Holland after she had sold her jewels to support his
cause, and set sail with just three ships and a few hundred men to seize
the throne of England. On 11 June 1685, he landed at Lyme in Dorset,
raised his blue banner, and was proclaimed King at Taunton. On 6th
July James II's regular army met Monmouth's straggling forces at
Sedgemoor and crushed them. On 15 July, after a grovelling plea to his
uncle, Monmouth died bravely on Tower Hill, telling the executioner
that his blade was not sharp enough – which proved to be right, as it
took seven strokes to kill him.

JUDGE JEFFREYS

A True Englishman

Let a lewd judge come reeking from a wench
To vent a wilder lust upon the bench;
Bawl out the venom of his rotten heart,
Swell'd up with envy, over-act his part;
Condemn the innocent by laws ne'er fram'd
And study to be more than doubly damn'd.
                                    Anonymous

Judge Jeffreys was made Lord Chief Justice in 1683 after presiding over the trial of Titus Oates. James II made him Lord Chancellor, and in the aftermath of Sedgemoor he conducted what came to be known as the Bloody Assizes in the West Country.

1688

THE TRIAL OF THE SEVEN BISHOPS

The Song of the Western Men

A good sword and a trusty hand!
   A merry heart and true!
King James's men shall understand
   What Cornish lads can do.

And have they fixed the where and when?
   And shall Trelawny die?
Here's twenty thousand Cornish men
   Will know the reason why!

Out spake their captain brave and bold,
   A merry wight was he:
'If London Tower were Michael's hold,
   We'll set Trelawny free!

We'll cross the Tamar, land to land,
   The Severn is no stay,
With 'one and all', and hand in hand,
   And who shall bid us nay?

And when we come to London Wall,
   A pleasant sight to view,
Come forth! come forth, ye cowards all,
   Here's men as good as you!

Trelawny he's in keep and hold,
   Trelawny he may die;
But twenty thousand Cornish bold
Will know the reason why.'

            R. S. Hawker

Trelawny was the Bishop of Bristol, and one of the seven bishops to defy James and be imprisoned in the Tower. On the evening of their acquittal, seven English magnates signed an invitation to William of Orange to become their King and establish 'free Parliaments and the Protestant religion' in the land. Hawker was the nineteenth-century vicar of Morwenstow in Cornwall and became the most celebrated Cornish poet.

William and Mary, 1688–1702

WILLIAM III'S VIEW OF HIMSELF

As I walk'd by my self
And talk'd to my self,
My self said unto me,
Look to thy self,
Take care of thy self,
For nobody cares for Thee.

I answer'd my self,
And said to my self,
In the self-same Repartee,
Look to thy self
Or not look to thy self,
The self-same thing will be.

William III

On 5 November 1688, William, Prince of Orange, landed at Torbay in Devon, not far from where Monmouth had landed three years earlier. James II's army outnumbered his by two to one, but at Salisbury the King was incapacitated by severe nose-bleeding and decided not to march against William at Exeter. This delay was a great mistake. His military commander, John Churchill, defected, and James fled back to London where he threw the Great Seal of England into the Thames. He never put up a fight.

1689

Bonnie Dundee

To the Lords of Convention 'twas Claver'se who spoke,
'Ere the King's crown shall fall there are crowns to be broke;
Then each cavalier who loves honour and me,
Let him follow the bonnet of Bonnie Dundee.
  'Come fill up my cup, come fill up my can,

Come saddle your horses, and call up your men;
Come open the West Port, and let me gang free,
And it's room for the bonnets of Bonnie Dundee!'

Dundee he is mounted, he rides up the street,
The bells are rung backward, the drums they are beat;
But the Provost, douce man, said, 'Just e'en let him be,
The Guide Town is weel quit o' that De'il of Dundee.'
   'Come fill up my cup,' etc.

'There are hills beyond Pentland, and lands beyond Forth.
If there's lords in the Lowlands, there's chiefs in the north;
There are wild Duniewassals, three thousand times three,
Will cry 'hoigh!' for the bonnet of Bonnie Dundee.
   'Come fill up my cup,' etc.

'Away to the hills, to the caves, to the rocks –
Ere I own an unsurper. I'll couch with the fox;
And tremble, false Whigs, in the midst of your glee.
You have not seen the last of my bonnet and me.
   'Come fill up my cup,' etc.

Walter Scott

The Convention was the Parliamentary assembly which formalized the abdication of James II. There the Presbyterians of the Scottish Lowlands, who had been persecuted under James, were glad to proclaim William as the new King. The leader of the Catholics, Claverhouse, Viscount Dundee, rode out of the West Port of Edinburgh to raise the Highlands in the Stuart cause. The King's troops marched north to capture Blair Atholl Castle, but were met in the narrow pass of Killiecrankie by the Highlanders, who charged down upon the Redcoats only half an hour before sunset. Their heavy Claymores cut through the Royalist army, which withdrew to Stirling. At the moment of victory, however, 'Bonny' Dundee was shot and killed, as some said, by a silver bullet.

1690

THE BATTLE OF THE BOYNE

from **The Boyne Water**

July the First, of a morning clear, one thousand six hundred
    and ninety,
King William did his men prepare, of thousands he had thirty;
To fight King James and all his foes, encamped near the Boyne
    Water,
He little fear'd though two to one, their multitudes to scatter.

King William call'd his officers, saying: 'Gentlemen, mind your
    station,
And let your valour here be shown before this Irish nation;
My brazen walls let no man break, and your subtle foes you'll
    scatter,
Be sure you show them good English play as you go over the
    water.'

Within four yards of our fore-front, before a shot was fired,
A sudden snuff they got that day, which little they desired;
For horse and man fell to the ground, and some hung in their
    saddle;

Others turn'd up their forked ends, which we call 'coup de
ladle'.

Prince Eugene's regiment was the next, on our right hand
    advanced,
Into a field of standing wheat, where Irish horses pranced –
But the brandy ran so in their heads, their senses all did scatter,
They little thought to leave their bones that day at the Boyne
    Water.

Both men and horse lay on the ground, and many there lay
    bleeding;
I saw no sickles there that day – but, sure, there was sharp
    shearing.

So praise God, all true Protestants, and I will say no further,
But had the Papists gain'd the day there would have been open
    murder.
Although King James and many more were ne'er that way
    inclined,
It was not in their power to stop what the rabble they designed.

Anonymous

Three months after William had landed in England, James left France to
lead a rising of his supporters in Ireland. He laid siege to Londonderry,
which bravely held out for fifteen weeks, and then had to withdraw to
Dublin where he was reinforced by 6,000 French troops. William
landed in the north and marched on Dublin, but found his path blocked
by James's army where it was drawn up by the River Boyne, in a strong
defensive position. However, William's 36,000 soldiers crossed the river
and defeated James's 25,000. It proved a decisive victory, for it
established the ascendancy of the Protestant minority all over Ireland,
until the forces unleashed by the French Revolution led to the call for an
independent Catholic Ireland.

1701

THE EXECUTION OF CAPTAIN KIDD

Great Black-backed Gulls

Said Cap'n Morgan to Cap'n Kidd:
'Remember the grand times, Cap'n, when
The Jolly Roger flapped on the tropic breeze,
And we were the terrors of the Spanish Main?'
And Cap'n Kidd replied: 'Aye when our restless souls
Were steeped in human flesh and bone;
But now we range the seven seas, and fight
For galley scraps that men throw overboard.'

Two black-backed gulls, that perched
On a half-sunken spar –
Their eyes were gleaming-cold and through
The morning fog that crept upon the grey-green waves
Their wicked laughter sounded.

John Heath-Stubbs

Sir Henry Morgan and William Kidd were the two most notorious
pirates of the Spanish Main. They plundered the merchant ships
engaged in the circular trade of slaves from Africa and sugar to Europe.
Morgan died as Lieutenant-Governor of Jamaica, but Kidd was hanged
at Execution Dock on the Thames in 1701.

1702

THE DEATH OF WILLIAM III

But William had not Govern'd Fourteen Year,
To be an unconcern'd Spectator here:
His Works like Providence were all Compleat,
And made a Harmony we Wonder'd at.
The Legislative Power he set Free,
And led them step by step to Liberty,
'Twas not his Fault if they cou'd not Agree.
Impartial Justice He protected so,
The Laws did in their Native Channels flow,
From whence our sure Establishment begun,
And William laid the first Foundation Stone:
On which the stately Fabrick soon appear'd,
How cou'd they sink when such a Pilot steer'd?
He taught them due defences to prepare,
And make their future Peace their present care:
By him directed, Wisely they Decreed,
What Lines shou'd be expell'd, and what succeed;
That now he's Dead, there's nothing to be done,
But to take up the Scepter he laid down.

Daniel Defoe

William served England well, but by the winter of 1701 he was worn out and did not expect to see another summer. In February 1702 his horse, Sorrel, stumbled, it is said, on a mole hill, and threw the King off, breaking his collar-bone. Within three weeks he was dead. He had never been a popular figure: people did not like his asthmatic cough, his hooked nose, his solitariness, or the fact that he was foreign. Defoe tried to set the record straight.

Queen Anne, 1702–14

from An Ode Humbly Inscrib'd to the Queen

But, Greatest *Anna*! while Thy Arms pursue
Paths of Renown, and climb Ascents of Fame
Which nor *Augustus* nor *Eliza* knew;
What *Poet* shall be found to sing Thy Name?
What Numbers shall Record? What Tongue shall say
Thy Wars on Land, Thy Triumphs on the Main?
Oh Fairest Model of Imperial Sway!
What Equal Pen shall write Thy wond'rous Reign?
Who shall Attempts and Victories rehearse
By Story yet untold, unparallell'd by Verse?

Matthew Prior

Anne ruled for twelve years and, for eleven of those, British armies were busy fighting Louis XIV and winning great victories. The politics of Anne's reign were Byzantine, but they saw the consolidation of identifiable groupings of Whigs and Tories. It was a glittering period in terms of military and literary achievement, but the Queen herself remains a shadowy figure. The most people are able to say about her is that 'Queen Anne is dead'. In 1712 her statue was erected outside St Paul's and there it stands to this day. As an anonymous squib-writer put it:

> Brandy Nan, Brandy Nan,
> You're left in the lurch
> With your face to the gin shop
> And your back to the Church.

1704

THE BATTLE OF BLENHEIM

from **After Blenheim**

'Twas a summer evening,
　　Old Kaspar's work was done,
And he before his cottage door
　　Was sitting in the sun,
And by him sported on the green
His little grandchild, Wilhelmine.

She saw her brother Peterkin
　　Roll something large and round,
Which he beside the rivulet
　　In playing there had found;
He came to ask what he had found
That was so large, and smooth, and round.

Old Kaspar took it from the boy
　　Who stood expectant by;
And then the old man shook his hand.
　　And with a natural sigh –
' 'Tis some poor fellow's skull,' said he,
'Who fell in that great victory.'

'I find them in the garden,
　　For there's many here about;
And often when I go to plough
　　The ploughshare turns them out.
For many thousand men,' said he,
'Were slain in that great victory.'

'Now tell us what 'twas all about,'
　　Young Peterkin, he cries;
And little Wilhelmine looks up
　　With wonder-waiting eyes;
'Now tell us all about the war,
And what they fought each other for.'

'It was the English,' Kaspar cried,
  'Who put the French to rout;
But what they fought each other for
  I could not well make out;
But everybody said,' quoth he,
'That 'twas a famous victory.

'And everybody praised the Duke
  Who this great fight did win.'
'But what good came of it at last?'
  Quoth little Peterkin.
'Why, that I cannot tell,' said he,
'But 'twas a famous victory.'

Robert Southey

The Duke of Marlborough led a huge army of English and European troops on the long march from Cologne to Austria, where one of Louis XIV's armies was threatening to capture the Habsburg capital, Vienna. A battle was fought over a three-mile front and through the village of Blenheim, between armies of much the same size – about 60,000 men each. It was indeed a bloody contest, for about half of the French force was killed. After seventeen hours in the saddle, Marlborough was able to scribble a note on the back of a tavern bill: 'Let the Queen know, her Army has had a Glorious Victory.'

On Sir John Vanbrugh

Under this stone, reader, survey
Dead Sir John Vanbrugh's house of clay.
Lie heavy on him, earth! for he
Laid many heavy loads on thee.

Abel Evans

In 1705 the Queen, with the consent of Parliament, granted her Captain-General Marlborough the royal manor of Woodstock – 16,000 acres on which Marlborough asked Sir John Vanbrugh, the playwright and architect, to build him a palace.

HAMPTON COURT

from **The Rape of the Lock**

Close by those meads, for ever crowned with flowers
Where Thames with pride surveys his rising towers,
There stands a structure of majestic frame,
Which from the neighb'ring Hampton takes its name.
Here Britain's statesmen oft the fall foredoom
Of foreign tyrants and of nymphs at home;
Here thou, great Anna! whom three realms obey,
Dost sometimes counsel take – and sometimes tea.
Hither the heroes and the nymphs resort,
To taste awhile the pleasures of a court;
In various talk the instructive hours they passed,
Who gave the ball, or paid the visit last;
One speaks the glory of the British Queen,
And one describes a charming Indian screen;
A third interprets motions, looks, and eyes;
At every word a reputation dies.
Snuff, or the fan, supply each pause of chat,
With singing, laughing, ogling, and all that.
Meanwhile, declining from the noon of day,
The sun obliquely shoots his burning ray;
The hungry judges soon the sentence sign,
And wretches hang that jury-men may dine;
The merchant from the Exchange returns in peace,
And the long labours of the toilet cease.

Alexander Pope

Christopher Wren had designed a great and elegant extension to the Tudor palace of Hampton Court. William III and Queen Anne both spent a lot of time there, and their courtiers indulged in the comparatively new fashion of taking tea. Tea, coffee and cocoa were introduced to England in the middle of the seventeenth century. The East India Company had been given the monopoly of trade to the Far East and by Queen Anne's reign it had pushed the Dutch into second place. Thousands of tons of tea were imported each year, with porcelain as a makeweight, and at its height tea accounted for 5 per cent of British imports. Britain was well on its way to becoming a nation of tea-drinkers. The tea which Queen Anne drank came from China, for Indian tea reached these shores only as late as 1840, and she would have drunk it from a Chinese bowl without handles – these were not added until 1750.

THE HANOVERIAN HEIR

The crown's far too weighty
For shoulders of eighty;
She could not sustain such a trophy;
Her hand, too, already
Has grown so unsteady
She can't hold a sceptre;
So Providence kept her
Away. – Poor old Dowager Sophy.
Thomas D'Urfey

Queen Anne's seven children had all died. The last, a boy, the Duke of Gloucester, was born in 1689. When he died in 1700 Parliament passed the Act of Settlement which named the ageing Sophia Dorothea, Electress and Dowager Duchess of Hanover, as Anne's successor since she was a Protestant. Anne did not care for this distant relative, and D'Urfey got fifty guineas as a reward for singing her the song from which this snatch is taken. As it happened, Sophia died before Anne, and so her son, George, succeeded.

The Hanoverians, 1715–1837

George I, a German prince, became King of England in 1715 because only a Protestant could succeed to the throne. The Protestant succession was challenged by the Catholic Stuarts; in the first Jacobite rebellion of 1715 and the second by Bonnie Prince Charlie in 1745. Both were decisively defeated.

George I could not speak English and his son, George II, spent much of his reign in his continental possession of Hanover. This semi-absentee kingship meant that a prime minister, notably Robert Walpole, led the government. Parliament became more powerful and towards the end of the period the Great Reform Bill of 1832 laid the foundation for the democratic system of the nineteenth and twentieth centuries.

The foundations of the British Empire were laid when the French forces were defeated in India by Robert Clive and in Canada by General Wolfe. However, the American colonies broke away in their War of Independence in the 1770s.

William Pitt the Elder galvanized Britain in the Seven Years' War and his son, William Pitt the Younger, rallied Europe to resist the revolutionary armies of France in 1792 and the imperial ambitions of Napoleon from 1800. Britain was the only country in Europe that was not conquered by Napoleon. He was eventually defeated at the Battle of Waterloo in 1815 by the combined armies of Britain and Russia.

During the eighteenth century the inventive genius of such engineers as James Watt, Richard Arkwright and Robert Stevenson, who designed and built the first steam train, gave birth to the Industrial Revolution.

It was a glorious period for music, painting, literature and architecture. Alexander Pope, Dean Swift and George Frederick Handel dominated the first forty years and the Romantic movement was launched in 1798 by William Wordsworth and Samuel Taylor Coleridge with *The Lyrical Ballads*, paving the way for Keats, Shelley and Byron. The first English novel was written by Samuel Richardson, and it became an art form through the works of Walter Scott and Jane Austen. The great houses of England and Scotland, designed by Robert Adams and John Nash, housed the paintings of Gainsborough, Turner and Reynolds, and the furniture of Chippendale and Sheraton. It was a golden age.

King George I, 1714–27

George I – Star of Brunswick

He preferr'd Hanover to England,
He preferr'd two hideous mistresses
To a beautiful and innocent wife.
He hated arts and despised literature;
But he liked train-oil in his salads,
And gave an enlighten'd patronage to bad oysters.
And he had Walpole as a minister;
Consistent in his preference for every kind of corruption.

H. J. Daniel

At the age of fifty-four, George, the Elector of Hanover, came to the throne of a country he had never visited, whose language he never spoke and whose people he never loved. He had divorced his wife, the mother of George II, twenty years earlier and he brought with him his long established mistress, Melusine von der Schulenberg, who had borne him three daughters and was later made the Duchess of Kendal. It was also alleged that he had another mistress, his half-sister, Sophie Charlotte, who became the Countess of Darlington. As Kendal was tall and thin, and Darlington was short and fat, they were known as 'The Maypole and the Elephant'.

1715

THE FIRST JACOBITE UPRISING

A Jacobite's Epitaph

To my true king I offered free from stain
Courage and faith; vain faith, and courage vain.
For him I threw lands, honours, wealth, away,
And one dear hope, that was more prized then they.
For him I languished in a foreign clime,
Grey-haired with sorrow in my manhood's prime;
Heard on Lavernia Scargill's whispering trees,
And pined by Arno for my lovelier Tees;

Beheld each night my home in fevered sleep,
Each morning started from the dream to weep;
Till God, who saw me tried too sorely, gave
The resting-place I asked, an early grave.
O thou, whom chance leads to this nameless stone,
From that proud country which was once mine own,
By those white cliffs I never more must see,
By that dear language which I spake like thee,
Forget all feuds, and shed one English tear.
O'er English dust. A broken heart lies here.

Thomas Babington, Lord Macaulay

The Stuart cause was kept alive by the son of James II. Known as the
Old Pretender and kept in Paris by the favour of Louis XIV, he became
the hope of all malcontents in England. And he failed them all. Nine
months after the accession of George I, he encouraged the Earl of Mar
to raise a rebellion in the Highlands. It was a botched and bungled
affair and, although some rebels reached Preston, they were trounced
and fled northwards again. James himself eventually arrived in Perth
just in time to retreat to Dundee, and within four weeks he was back in
France, before finally settling in Italy.

1727

THE DEATH OF SIR ISAAC NEWTON

from To the Memory of Sir Isaac Newton

Even *Light itself*, which every thing displays,
Shone undiscover'd, till his brighter mind
Untwisted all the shining robe of day;
And, from the whitening undistinguish'd blaze,
Collecting every ray into his kind,
To the charm'd eye educ'd the gorgeous train
Of *Parent-Colours*. First the flaming *Red*
Sprung vivid forth; the tawny *Orange* next;
And next delicious *Yellow*; by whose side
Fell the kind beams of all-refreshing *Green*.
Then the pure *Blue*, that swells autumnal skies,

Ethereal play'd; and then, of sadder hue,
Emerg'd the deepen'd *Indico*, as when
The heavy-skirted evening droops with frost.
While the last gleamings of refracted light
Dy'd in the fainting *Violet* away.
These, when the clouds distil the rosy shower,
Shine out distinct adown the watry bow;
While o'er our heads the dewy vision bends
Delightful, melting on the fields beneath.
Myriads of mingling dies from these result,
And myriads still remain – Infinite source
Of beauty, ever-flushing, ever-new!
    Did ever poet image ought so fair,
Dreaming in whispering groves, by the hoarse brook!
Or prophet, to whose rapture heaven descends!
Even now the setting sun and shifting clouds,
Seen, *Greenwich*, from thy lovely heights, declare
How just, how beauteous the *refractive Law*.

James Thomson

Newton was a genius in mathematics, physics, astronomy and philosophy. His great works were *Philosophiae naturalis principia mathematica* (1687) and *Opticks* (1704). He formulated the Law of Gravity and the three Laws of Motion, established that white light consists of a mixture of all colours, and developed calculus. Voltaire, who was at Newton's funeral, commended the English for honouring a scientist of heretical religious views with burial in Westminster Abbey. Einstein's view of Newton was that he 'determined the course of Western thought, research and practice to an extent that nobody before or since can touch'.

Epitaph Intended for Sir Isaac Newton, in Westminster Abbey

Nature, and Nature's laws lay hid in night:
God said, *Let Newton be!* and all was light.

Alexander Pope

It did not last: the Devil howling 'Ho!
Let Einstein be!' restored the status quo.

J. C. Squire

King George II, 1727–60

In most things I did as my father had done,
I was false to my wife and I hated my son:
My spending was small, and my avarice much,
My kingdom was English, my heart was High-Dutch:
At Dettingen fight I was not known to blench,
I butcher'd the Scotch, and I bearded the French:
I neither had morals, nor manners, nor wit;
I wasn't much miss'd when I died in a fit.
Here set up my statue, and make it complete,
With Pitt on his knees at my dirty old feet.

H. J. Daniel

George II had been bullied by his father, and in turn he tried to bully his son. He was lucky to have a loving and clever wife, Caroline. Walpole used the Queen to persuade the King to support his policies, or, as he put it in his earthy Norfolk way, he 'took the right sow by the ear'. George II was the last monarch to lead a British army to victory, which he did at Dettingen in Bavaria. He liked all things military and was able to recall in detail the uniforms of European regiments. His great love, however, was music, and he made it possible for the German composer George Frederick Handel to live in England. In his will he asked that his coffin be laid alongside that of his wife, with the two near sides open so that their dusts might mingle.

SIR ROBERT WALPOLE

A Character Study

With favour and fortune fastidiously blest,
He's loud in his laugh and he's coarse in his jest;
Of favour and fortune unmerited vain,
A sharper in trifles, a dupe in the main.
Achieving of nothing, still promising wonders,
By dint of experience improving in blunders;
Oppressing true merit, exalting the base,

And selling his country to purchase his peace.
A jobber of stocks by retailing false news,
A prater at court in the style of the stews,
Of virtue and worth by profession a giber,
Of juries and senates the bully and briber:
Though I name not the wretch you know who I mean –
'Tis the cur dog of Britain and spaniel of Spain.

Jonathan Swift

Walpole was Prime Minister from 1721 to 1742, which is a record yet to
be surpassed. His policy was, proverbially, to let sleeping dogs lie – to
avoid war, encourage trade and reduce taxation. He exercised
enormous patronage, finding so many jobs for his sons, brothers,
cousins and friends that his administration came to be known as the
'Robinocracy'. He was also the last PM to make a huge personal fortune
while in office: government surpluses passed though his own account
and enabled him to speculate on a grand scale. He collected some
superb paintings, which one of his descendants sold to Catherine the
Great of Russia and which now form the heart of the Hermitage
Museum in St Petersburg. He gave England peace for eighteen years;
he reinforced the power of the House of Commons; he consolidated the
achievements of the Whig revolution; and he eliminated from politics
the savagery and vindictiveness which in previous generations could
lead those who had fallen on misfortune to the gallows or into exile.
Swift saw Walpole as the barrier to his preferment in England, and
loathed him for it.

1739

THE LAST DAYS OF DICK TURPIN

My Poor Black Bess

When fortune, blind goddess, she fled my abode,
Old friends proved ungrateful, I took to the road;
To plunder the wealthy to aid my distress,
I bought thee to aid me, my poor Black Bess.

When dark sable night its mantle had thrown
O'er the bright face of nature, how oft we have gone

To famed Hounslow Heath, though an unwelcome guest
To the minions of fortune, my poor Black Bess.

How silent thou stood when a carriage I've stopped,
And their gold and their jewels its inmates I've dropped;
No poor man I plundered or e'er did oppress
The widow or orphan, my poor Black Bess.

When Argus-eyed justice did me hotly pursue,
From London to York like lightning we flew;
No toll-bar could stop thee, thou the river didst breast,
And in twelve hours reached it, my poor Black Bess.

Anonymous

Tradition has transformed Dick Turpin into romantic figure, but in real
life he was no more than a poacher, thief, highwayman and murderer.
He did not even make the famous twelve-hour ride to York which has
been attributed to him: that was the feat of another highwayman in
1676. For a while, Turpin lived in York under the name of Palmer, but
he was discovered after a quarrel with an innkeeper over a gamecock.
He was executed in 1739, having paid five people to mourn for him.

1740

THE GROWTH OF THE BRITISH EMPIRE

from **The Masque of Alfred**

When Britain first at Heaven's command
  Arose from out the azure main,
This was the charter of the land,
  And guardian angels sang this strain,
    'Rule Britannia, rule the waves,
    Britons never will be slaves.

'The nations not so blest as thee
  Must in their turn to tyrants fall,
While thou shalt flourish great and free,
  The dread and envy of them all.

'Still more majestic shalt thou rise,
  More dreadful from each foreign stroke;
As the loud blast that tears the skies
  Serves but to root thy native oak.

'Thee haughty tyrants ne'er shall tame;
  All their attempts to bend thee down
Will but arouse thy generous flame,
  But work their woe and thy renown.

'To thee belongs the rural reign,
  Thy cities shall with commerce shine;
All thine shall be the subject main,
  And every shore it circles thine.

'The muses, still with freedom found,
  Shall to thy happy coast repair;
Blest Isle! with matchless beauty crowned,
  And manly hearts to guard the fair!
    'Rule, Britannia, rule the waves,
    Britons never will be slaves.'
                              James Thomson

George II's reign saw the steady expansion and consolidation of the British Empire, although only one new colony was founded, namely Georgia, which was initially settled by debtors from the Fleet Prison. In the 1750s British armies won sweeping victories in Europe, as well as in India under Clive and in Canada under Wolfe.

1745

THE SECOND JACOBITE UPRISING

Charlie is my Darling

Charlie is my darling, my darling, my darling,
Charlie is my darling, the young Chevalier.

'Twas on a Monday morning,
    Right early in the year,
When Charlie came to our toun,
    The young Chevalier.

As he came marching up the street,
    The pipes played loud and clear,
And a' the folk came running out
    To meet the Chevalier.

We' Hieland bonnets on their heads,
    And claymores bright and clear,
They came to fight for Scotland's right,
    And the young Chevalier.

They've left their bonnie Hieland hills,
    Their wives and bairnies dear,
To draw the sword for Scotland's lord,
    The young Chevalier.

Oh, there were mony beating hearts,
    And mony a hope and fear:
And mony were the pray'rs put up
    For the young Chevalier.

                                        Lady Nairne

In July 1745 Prince Charles Edward Stuart, the Young Pretender, landed in Scotland with the intention of recapturing the three kingdoms lost by his grandfather, James II. He had no troops with him, no money, and only seven friends. The Highland clans, led by the Macdonalds, rallied to him, and by September he had entered Edinburgh and won the skirmish of Prestonpans. Then he made the mistake of marching into England, passing through Preston and Manchester, and finally reaching Derby, where his men refused to go further. England failed to rally to him and he retreated north, pursued by the Duke of Cumberland.

1746

THE BATTLE OF CULLODEN

Lament for Culloden

The lovely lass o' Inverness,
Nae joy nor pleasure can she see;
For e'en and morn she cries, Alas!
And aye the saut tear blins her ee:
Drumossie moor – Drumossie day –
A waefu' day it was to me!
For there I lost my father dear,
My father dear, and brethren three.

Their winding-sheet the bluidy clay,
Their graves are growing green to see:
And by them lies the dearest lad
That ever blest a woman's ee!
Now wae to thee, thou cruel lord,
A bluidy man I trow thou be,
For mony a heart thou hast made sair
That ne'er did wrang to thine or thee.

Robert Burns

In 1746 the opposing armies met at Culloden, where Cumberland's 9,000 men ran down and slaughtered Charles's 5,000. For five months the Prince wandered through the Highlands, sheltered by poor crofters and rescued at one point by the now famous Flora Macdonald, but at last he returned to the Continent. The whole rash escapade had been poorly planned, poorly financed and poorly conducted. It was sustained by a romantic myth, but it led to the deaths of many thousands of Scots at the hands of 'Butcher' Cumberland. A flower in England is called Sweet William but the Scots named a weed Stinking Billy in memory of his savage reprisals.

SEA POWER

Heart of Oak

Come cheer up my lads, 'tis to glory we steer,
To add something new to this wonderful year;
To honour we call you, not press you like slaves,
For who are so free as the sons of the waves?

Heart of Oak are our ships, Heart of Oak are our men,
    We always are ready,
    Steady, boys, steady,
We'll fight and we'll conquer again and again.

We ne'er meet our foes but we wish them to stay,
They ne'er meet us but they wish us away;
If they run, then we follow, and drive them ashore,
For if they won't fight us, we cannot do more.
    Heart of Oak, &c.

They talk to invade us, these terrible foes,
They frighten our women, our children, and beaux;
But, if their flat bottoms in darkness come o'er,
Sure Britons they'll find to receive them on shore.
    Heart of Oak, &c.

We'll make them to run, and we'll make them to sweat,
In spite of the Devil and Russel's Gazette;
Then cheer up my lads, with one heart let us sing,
Our soldiers, our sailors, our statesmen, our king.
    Heart of Oak, &c.

David Garrick

The great actor-manager David Garrick wrote this song for his pantomime, *Harlequin's Invasion*, to celebrate British victories over the French at Lagos, Quiberon Bay and Quebec.

WRECKING

Song of the Cornish Wreckers

Not that they shall, but if they must –
Be just, Lord, wreck them off St Just.

Scythes beneath the water, Brisons,
Reap us a good crop in all seasons.

We would be meek, but meat we lack,
Pile wrecks on Castle Kenidjack.

Our children's mouths gape like a zawn.
Fog, hide the sharp fangs of Pendeen.

You put Your own Son first, Jehovah,
And so do we. Send bread to Morvah.

Crowbar of oceans, stove the wood
Treasure-troves on Gurnard's Head.

Mermaids, Mary-Anne, Morwenna,
Sing them to the crags of Zennor.

Food, Lord, food! Our starving flock
Looks for manna but finds a rock.

Hard land you give us. Mist and stones.
Not enough trees to bury our bones.

To save the drowning we'll risk our lives.
But hurl their ships upon St Ives.

Guide us, when through death we sail,
Past the burning cliffs of Hell.

Soul nor sailor mean we harm.
But our blue sky is their black storm.

D. M. Thomas

In the eighteenth century British sailors ruled the seas, dominating trade, extending empire and beating off all comers in the competition for naval supremacy. These two poems show the darker side of things – the business of wrecking and smuggling. The places mentioned in Thomas's poem are on the north-west coast of Cornwall, near to Land's End. There was a medieval law which stated that the goods salvaged from a wreck belonged to those who got possession of them. Some ships were lured on to the rocks by false beacons, and when in trouble were followed along the cliff-tops by entire village communities, ready to pounce on what floated ashore. Sailors escaping a wreck knew that they would also have to flee the locals, who would be quite prepared to push them under as they grabbed what was going.

SMUGGLING

A Smuggler's Song

If you wake at midnight, and hear a horse's feet,
Don't go drawing back the blind, or looking in the street
Them that ask no questions isn't told a lie.
Watch the wall, my darling, while the Gentlemen go by!
    Five and twenty ponies,
    Trotting through the dark –
    Brandy for the Parson,
    'Baccy for the Clerk;

Laces for a lady, letters for a spy,
And watch the wall, my darling, while the Gentlemen go by!

Running round the woodlump if you chance to find
Little barrels, roped and tarred, all full of brandy-wine,
Don't you shout to come and look, nor use 'em for your play.
Put the brushwood back again – and they'll be gone next day!

If you see the stable-door setting open wide;
If you see a tired horse lying down inside;
If your mother mends a coat cut about and tore;
If the lining's wet and warm – don't you ask no more!

If you meet King George's men, dressed in blue and red,
You be careful what you say, and mindful what is said.
If they call you 'pretty maid,' and chuck you 'neath the chin,
Don't you tell where no one is, nor yet where no one's been!

Knocks and footsteps round the house – whistles after dark –
You've no call for running out till the house-dogs bark.
Trusty's here, and *Pincher*'s here, and see how dumb they lie –
They don't fret to follow when the Gentlemen go by!

If you do as you've been told, 'likely there's a chance,
You'll be given a dainty doll, all the way from France,
With a cap of Valenciennes, and a velvet hood –
A present from the Gentlemen, along o' being good!
    Five and twenty ponies,
    Trotting through the dark –
    Brandy for the Parson,
    'Baccy for the Clerk;
Them that asks no questions isn't told a lie –
Watch the wall, my darling, while the Gentlemen go by!

                                        Rudyard Kipling

King George III, 1760–1820

George the Third
Ought never to have occurred.
One can only wonder
At so grotesque a blunder.

E. C. Bentley

George III himself was a conscientious but inadequate monarch. He had fifteen children, more than any other British king, but was sadly let down by his sons, for they proved a gaggle of spendthrifts, drunkards and adulterers. He suffered from bouts of madness and was permanently insane for the last eleven years of his reign. He had what has now been diagnosed as porphyria, which can now be treated, but he was forced to endure seclusion and strait-jackets. His doctors did also advise him to bathe in the sea for therapeutic purposes, which started the fashion of the seaside holiday.

A PORTRAIT OF THE KING

from Mr Whitbread's Brewhouse

Now Majesty into a pump so deep
Did with an opera-glass so curious peep,
Examining with care each won'drous matter
    That brought up water!

Thus have I seen a magpie in the street,
A chatt'ring bird we often meet,
A bird for curiosity well known,
    With head awry,
    And cunning eye,
Peep knowingly into a marrow-bone.

And now his curious Majesty did stoop
To count the nails on ev'ry hoop;
And lo! no single one came in his way,
That, full of deep research, he did not say,

'What's this? hae, hae? what's that? what's this? what's that?'
So quick the words too, when he deign'd to speak,
As if each syllable would break its neck.

To Whitbread now deign's Majesty to say,
'Whitbread, are all your horses fond of hay?'
'Yes, please your Majesty,' in humble notes,
The Brewer answer'd – 'also, Sir, of oats:
Another thing my horses too maintains,
And that, an't please your Majesty, are grains.'

'Grains, grains,' said Majesty, 'to fill their crops?
Grains, grains? – that comes from hops – yes, hops, hops, hops?'

Here was the King, like hounds sometimes, at fault –
'Sire,' cry'd the humble Brewer, 'give me leave
Your sacred Majesty to undeceive:
Grains, Sire, are never made from hops, but malt.'

'True,' said the cautious Monarch, with a smile;
From malt, malt, malt – I meant malt all the while.'
'Yes,' with the sweetest now, rejoin'd the Brewer,
'An't please your Majesty, you did, I'm sure.'
'Yes,' answer'd Majesty, with quick reply,
'I did, I did, I did, I, I, I, I.'

Peter Pindar

Writing under the pseudonym of Peter Pindar, Devonshire clergyman
John Wolcot launched satirical attacks on the slow-wittedness of the
King, here depicted on a tour of Whitbread's Brewery in Islington.

1770

AGRICULTURAL DECLINE

from The Deserted Village

Sweet smiling village, loveliest of the lawn,
Thy sports are fled, and all thy charms withdrawn;
Amidst thy bowers the tyrant's hand is seen,

And desolation saddens all thy green:
One only master grasps the whole domain,
And half a tillage stintst thy smiling plain:
No more thy glassy brook reflects the day,
But chok'd with sedges, works its weedy way.
Along thy glades, a solitary guest,
The hollow-sounding bittern guards its nest;
Amidst thy desert walks the lapwing flies,
And tires their echoes with unvaried cries.
Sunk are thy bowers, in shapeless ruin all,
And the long grass o'ertops the mouldering wall;
And, trembling, shrinking from the spoiler's hand,
Far, far away, thy children leave the land.

Ill fares the land, to hastening ills a prey,
Where wealth accumulates, and men decay:
Princes and lords may flourish, or may fade;
A breath can make them, as a breath has made;
But a bold peasantry, their country's pride,
When once destroy'd, can never be supplied.

A time there was, ere England's griefs began,
When every rood of ground maintain'd its man;
For him light labour spread her wholesome store,
Just gave what life requir'd, but gave no more:
His best companions, innocence and health;
And his best riches, ignorance of wealth.

But times are alter'd; trade's unfeeling train
Usurp the land and dispossess the swain;
Along the lawn, where scatter'd hamlets rose,
Unwieldy wealth, and cumbrous pomp repose;
And every want to opulence allied,
And every pang that folly pays to pride.

Oliver Goldsmith

The Lincolnshire Poacher

When I was bound apprentice in famous Lincolnshire,
Full well I served my Master for more than seven year,
Till I took up with poaching, as you shall quickly hear:
Oh! 'tis my delight on a shiny night in the season of the year!

As me and my comrades were setting of a snare,
'Twas then we seed the gamekeeper – for him we did not care,
For we can wrestle and fight, my boys, and jump o'er
anywhere,
Oh! 'tis my delight, *etc.*

As me and my comrades were setting four or five,
And taking on him up again, we caught the hare alive;
We caught the hare alive, my boys, and through the woods did
steer:
Oh! 'tis my delight, *etc.*

I threw him on my shoulder, and then we trudged home,
We took him to a neighbour's house and sold him for a crown;
We sold him for a crown, my boys, but I did not tell you where,
Oh! 'tis my delight, *etc.*

Bad luck to every magistrate that lives in Lincolnshire,
Success to every poacher that wants to sell a hare;
Bad luck to every gamekeeper that will not sell his deer:
Oh! 'tis my delight, *etc.*

Anonymous

During George III's reign, poaching was such a menace that more than fifty statutes were passed in the effort to suppress it. Yet as more and more common land was enclosed, the rural poor had increasing need to practise it. Heavy sentences were passed, and even the death penalty was applied, but with the discovery of Australia a new possibility arose, and English magistrates started to populate the colony with poachers. This folk song became a favourite of George IV, probably because he enjoyed neither shooting nor hunting.

1775

THE AMERICAN WAR OF INDEPENDENCE

Concord Hymn

By the rude bridge that arched the flood,
    Their flag to April's breeze unfurled,
Here once the embattled farmers stood,
    And fired the shot heard round the world.

The foe long since in silence slept;
    Alike the conqueror silent sleeps;
And Time the ruined bridge has swept
    Down the dark stream which seaward creeps.

On this green bank, by this soft stream,
    We set to-day a votive stone;
That memory may their deed redeem,
    When, like our sires, our sons are gone.

Spirit, that made those heroes dare
    To die, or leave their children free,
Bid Time and Nature gently spare
    The shaft we raise to them and thee.

Ralph Waldo Emerson

In the 1770s Lord North's government, in an attempt to reassert the sovereignty of the English crown over the American colonies, which had shown an increasingly independent spirit, took various unpopular measures, including the levying of duty on tea. In London, Lord Chatham pleaded for moderation and the withdrawal of troops, and Edmund Burke in a famous speech declared: 'Magnanimity in politics is not seldom the truest wisdom, and a great Empire and little minds go ill together.' But in 1775 open conflict was inevitable. Massachusetts had armed its militia against the troops of the English general, Gage, who set out to seize its armoury at Concord. On the way there a skirmish took place at Lexington, and the first shots of the war were fired. Sixty Americans and 273 British soldiers were killed. In July George Washington was recognized as Commander-in-Chief of the rebels and a year later the Declaration of Independence was signed. In 1777 a British army under 'Gentleman Johnny' Burgoyne surrendered at Saratoga Springs, and in 1781 another, under Lord Cornwallis, surrendered at Yorktown.

1782

EIGHTEENTH-CENTURY CONSCRIPTION

The Press-gang

Oh, where will you hurry my dearest?
　Say, say, to what clime or what shore?
You tear him from me, the sincerest
　That ever lov'd mortal before.

Ah! cruel, hard-hearted to press him
　And force the dear youth from my arms!
Restore him, that I may caress him,
　And shield him from future alarms.

In vain you insult and deride me
　And make but a scoff of my woes;
You ne'er from my dear shall divide me –
　I'll follow wherever he goes.

Think not of the merciless ocean –
　My soul any terror can brave,
For soon as the ship makes its motion,
　so soon shall the sea be my grave.

Charles Dibdin

Service in the British navy was so unpopular that men had to be pressed into it. Recruiting parties toured the ports, seizing the gullible and the unemployed, drunk or sober. Through the invocation of an Elizabethan Vagrancy Act, the prisons were emptied to man the fleet. Merchant ships were stopped on the high seas and crew forcibly transferred. Such treatment was one of the major sources of discontent among the American colonies. It was remarkable that there were so few mutinies, although one that took place at the Nore in 1797 almost brought the war effort to an end. Impressment ceased in practice in 1815, and in law in 1853, with the introduction of the service system.

1792

THE DEATH OF SIR JOSHUA REYNOLDS

from Retaliation

Here Reynolds is laid and, to tell you my mind,
He has not left a better or wiser behind:
His pencil was striking, resistless and grand;
His manners were gentle, complying and bland;
Still born to improve us in every part,
His pencil our faces, his manners our heart;
To coxcombs averse, yet most civilly steering,
When they judged without skill he was still hard of hearing;
When they talked of their Raphaels, Correggios and stuff,
He shifted his trumpet and only took snuff.

Oliver Goldsmith

When Goldsmith died in 1774, it was found that he had written a series of sketches of his closest friends in the form of epitaphs. This is what he wrote about the great painter Joshua Reynolds. Reynolds had settled in London in 1753 and had come to dominate British painting. In 1768 he enhanced the status of his profession by establishing the Royal Academy, of which he was the first President. He was very deaf and much preferred the company of literary men like Samuel Johnson, Goldsmith and Burke to that of painters. When Goldsmith's death was announced, Edmund Burke burst into tears and Reynolds threw down his palette and stopped painting for the day.

1793

THE SLAVE TRADE

The Negro's Complaint

Forc'd from home, and all its pleasures,
　　Afric's coast I left forlorn;
To increase a stranger's treasures,
　　O'er the raging billows borne,
Men from England bought and sold me.
　　Paid my price in paltry gold;
But though theirs they have enroll'd me,
　　Minds are never to be sold.

Still in thought as free as ever,
　　What are England's rights, I ask,
Me from my delights to sever,
　　Me to torture, me to task?
Fleecy locks, and black complexion
　　Cannot forfeit nature's claim;
Skins may differ, but affection
　　Dwells in white and black the same.

Why did all-creating Nature
　　Make the plant for which we toil?
Sighs must fan it, tears must water,
　　Sweat of ours must dress the soil.
Think, ye masters, iron-hearted,
　　Lolling at your jovial boards;
Think how many backs have smarted
　　For the sweets your cane affords.

Is there, as ye sometimes tell us,
　　Is there one who reigns on high?
Has he bid you buy and sell us,
　　Speaking from his throne the sky?
Ask him, if your knotted scourges,
　　Matches, blood-extorting screws,

Are the means which duty urges
　　Agents of his will to use!

Hark! he answers – Wild tornadoes,
　　Strewing yonder sea with wrecks;
Wasting towns, plantations, meadows,
　　Are the voice with which he speaks.
He, foreseeing what vexations
　　Afric's sons should undergo,
Fix'd their tyrants' habitations
　　Where his whirlwinds answer – No.

By our blood in Afric wasted,
　　Ere our necks receiv'd the chain;
By the mis'ries we have tasted,
　　Crossing in your barks the main;
By our suff'ring since ye brought us
　　To the man-degrading mart;
All sustain'd by patience, taught us
　　Only by a broken heart:

Deem our nation brutes no longer
　　Till some reason ye shall find
Worthier of regard and stronger
　　Than the colour of our kind.

Slaves of gold, whose sordid dealings
Tarnish all your boasted pow'rs,
Prove that you have human feelings,
Ere you proudly question ours!

William Cowper

In the triangular trade-system of the eighteenth century, ships from Europe took cloth, salt and guns to West Africa, then slaves from Africa to the Caribbean, and lastly sugar from the Caribbean back to Europe. This trade was based upon Europe's addiction to sugar, and it was that addiction which required and sustained the appalling institution of slavery. More than twenty million slaves crossed the Atlantic and an even greater number died on the journey. One slave produced about a ton of sugar in the course of his lifetime. The Quakers were among the first to condemn slavery, and Dr Johnson proposed a toast at Oxford to 'success to the next revolt of the Negroes in the West Indies'.

In 1772, the great Chief Justice Lord Mansfield had given his judgment against slavery: 'The Black must go free.' Adam Smith condemned the traffic and William Wilberforce, Pitt's close friend, moved bill after bill to ban it. In 1807 the Ministry of All Talents passed an act banning the trade and British ships were deputed to see that this was observed. Yet the traffic continued, and it was not until 1833 that an act was passed to outlaw slavery in all British possessions. Even then a young MP, W. E. Gladstone, whose family had Caribbean interests, predicted evil consequences for the West Indies and for the slaves themselves.

1803

THE NAPOLEONIC WARS

The Berkshire Farmer's Thoughts on Invasion

So! Bonaparte's coming, as folks seem to say,
(But I hope to have time to get in my hay).
And while he's caballing, and making a parley,
Perhaps I shall house all my wheat and my barley.
    Fal la de ral, &c.

Then I shall have time to attend to my duty,
And keep the starved dogs from making a booty

Of what I've been toiling for, both late and early,
To support my old woman, whom I love so dearly.
    Fal la de ral, &c.

Then, there are my children, and some of them feeble,
I wish, from my soul, that they were more able
To assist their old father, in drubbing the knaves,
For we ne'er will submit to become their tame slaves.
    Fal la de ral, &c.

But then, there's son Dick, who is both strong and lusty,
And towards the French he is damnable crusty;
If you give him a pitchfork or any such thing,
He will fight till he's dead, in defence of his King.
    Fal la de ral, &c.

And I'll answer for Ned, too, he'll never give out;
He should eat no more bacon, if I had a doubt.
And wish every one, who's not staunch in the cause,
May ne'er get a bit more to put in their jaws.
    Fal la de ral, &c.

So you see, Bonaparte, how you are mistaken,
In your *big little* notions of stealing our bacon.
And your *straight way to London*, I this will you tell,
Your straight way to London is your short way to Hell.
    Fal la de ral, &c.

Anonymous

From 1793 to 1815 Britain was almost continually at war with France. Napoleon rapidly came to dominate the whole of Europe. It was the British navy under Horatio Nelson which checked the French advance on different fronts at the Battle of the Nile in 1798, and again at Copenhagen in 1801. In 1803 Napoleon was ready to invade England and, with a huge army of 160,000 men gathered in Northern France, he practised embarking and landing. Pitt, out of office since 1801, was recalled and the country prepared to meet the invasion.

1805

THE DEATH OF NELSON

At Viscount Nelson's lavish funeral,
    While the mob milled and yelled about the Abbey,
A General chatted with an Admiral:

'One of your Colleagues, Sir, remarked today
    That Nelson's *exit*, though to be lamented,
Falls not inopportunely, in its way.'

'He was a thorn in our flesh,' came the reply –
    'The most bird-witted, unaccountable,
Odd little runt that ever I did spy.

'One arm, one peeper, vain as Pretty Poll,
    A meddler, too, in foreign politics
And gave his heart in pawn to a plain moll.

'He would dare lecture us Sea Lords, and then
    Would treat his ratings as though men of honour
And play at leap-frog with his midshipmen!

'We tried to box him down, but up he popped,
    And when he'd banged Napoleon at the Nile
Became too much the hero to be dropped.

'You've heard that Copenhagen "blind eye" story?
    We'd tied him to Nurse Parker's apron-strings –
By G–d, he snipped them through and snatched the glory!'

'Yet,' cried the General, 'six-and-twenty sail
    Captured or sunk by him off Trafalgar –
That writes a handsome *finis* to the tale.'

'Handsome enough. The seas are England's now.
    That fellow's foibles need no longer plague us.
He died most creditably, I'll allow.'

'And, Sir, the secret of his victories?'
  'By his unServicelike, familiar ways, Sir,
He made the whole Fleet love him, damn his eyes!'
                                        Robert Graves

Nelson saved the day. In 1805 he commanded the force which destroyed the French and Spanish fleets off Cape Trafalgar. With his twenty-seven ships he out-manoeuvred, out-gunned and out-fought the considerably greater numbers against him, but died from a sniper's bullet in the hour of victory.

1809

THE BATTLE OF CORUNNA

The Burial of Sir John Moore after Corunna

Not a drum was heard, not a funeral note,
  As his corpse to the rampart we hurried;
Not a soldier discharged his farewell shot
  O'er the grave where our hero we buried.

We buried him darkly at dead of night,
  The sods with our bayonets turning,
By the struggling moonbeam's misty light
  And the lanthorn dimly burning.

No useless coffin enclosed his breast,
  Not in sheet or in shroud we wound him;
But he lay like a warrior taking his rest
  With his martial cloak around him.

Few and short were the prayers we said,
  And we spoke not a word of sorrow;
But we steadfastly gazed on the face that was dead,
  And we bitterly thought of the morrow.

We thought, as we hollowed his narrow bed
  And smoothed down his lonely pillow,
That the foe and the stranger would tread o'er his head,
  And we far away on the billow!

Lightly they'll talk of the spirit that's gone,
  And o'er his cold ashes upbraid him –
But little he'll reck, if they let him sleep on
  In the grave where a Briton has laid him.

But half of our heavy task was done
  When the clock struck the hour for retiring;
And we heard the distant and random gun
  That the foe was sullenly firing.

Slowly and sadly we laid him down,
  From the field of his fame fresh and gory;
We carved not a line, and we raised not a stone,
  But we left him alone with his glory.

Charles Wolfe

In 1808 Napoleon annexed Spain and installed one of his brothers as King. In reply, the Duke of Wellington led a British army from Portugal to victory at Vimiera, but Napoleon then burst into Spain with 200,000 veterans, captured Madrid and forced the British, now under the command of Sir John Moore, to retreat. They marched 250 miles in nineteen days. Moore fought a rearguard action at Corunna while what was left of his army embarked. It was the Dunkirk of the Peninsular Wars, which Wellington eventually won in 1814.

THE LUDDITES

Enoch Made Them – Enoch Shall Break Them

And night by night when all is still,
And the moon is hid behind the hill,
We forward march to do our will
  With hatchet, pike and gun!
Oh, the cropper lads for me,
The gallant lads for me,
Who with lusty stroke
The shear frames broke,
The cropper lads for me!

Great Enoch still shall lead the van
Stop him who dare! stop him who can!
Press forward every gallant man
    With hatchet, pike, and gun!
Oh, the cropper lads for me . . .

Anonymous

In 1811 the textile and hosiery trades were depressed for three reasons: the trade embargo imposed as a punishment upon America for supporting Napoleon had slashed exports; men's fashions were changing and the old fabrics were no longer in such heavy demand; and new machinery threatened the jobs of skilled craftsmen. Well-organized gangs went from village to village in Lancashire, Yorkshire and Nottinghamshire, breaking up machines. Many of the hammers they used for this task had been made by Enoch Taylor of Marsden, a blacksmith, who also manufactured the new frames, which gave rise to the slogan quoted above. The Government, rattled by the recent assassination of Prime Minister Spencer Perceval, declared frame-breaking a capital offence and sent 12,000 troops to police the North – more than Wellington had commanded in Spain four years earlier.

Song for the Luddites

As the Liberty lads o'er the sea
Bought their freedom, and cheaply, with blood,
    So we, boys, we
    Will die fighting, or live free,
And down with all kings but King Ludd!

When the web that we weave is complete,
And the shuttle exchanged for the sword,
    We will fling the winding sheet
    O'er the despot at our feet,
And dye it deep in the gore he has pour'd.

Though black as his heart its hue,
Since his veins are corrupted to mud,
    Yet this is the dew
    Which the tree shall renew
Of Liberty, planted by Ludd!

George Gordon, Lord Byron

Luddism remained fitfully alive for a few years, ending in an outburst in 1816. But it achieved little. As the war ended, trade picked up, wages rose and more machines were needed to meet higher demand. In 1817, in Yorkshire, there were at least sixty more gig mills, and 1,300 more mechanical shears, than there had been before the troubles. There was, of course, no such figure as General Ludd in reality. The Nottingham-shire men had adopted the name of a legendary apprentice, said to have broken his stocking frame after he had been unfairly punished by his father.

1815

THE BATTLE OF WATERLOO

from Childe Harold's Pilgrimage

There was a sound of revelry by night,
   And Belgium's Capital had gathered then
   Her Beauty and her Chivalry, and bright
   The lamps shone o'er fair women and brave men;
   A thousand hearts beat happily; and when
   Music arose with its voluptuous swell,
   Soft eyes looked love to eyes which spake again,
And all went merry as a marriage bell;
But hush! hark! a deep sound strikes like a rising knell!

Did ye not hear it? – No; 'twas but the wind,
   Or the car rattling o'er the stony street;
   On with the dance! let joy be unconfined;
   No sleep till morn, when Youth and Pleasure meet
   To chase the glowing Hours with flying feet –
   But hark – that heavy sound breaks in once more,
   As if the clouds its echo would repeat;
   And nearer, clearer, deadlier than before!
Arm! Arm! it is – it is – the cannon's opening roar!

And there was mounting in hot haste: the steed,
   The mustering squadron, and the clattering car,
   Went pouring forward with impetuous speed,
   And swiftly forming in the ranks of war;

And the deep thunder peal on peal afar;
And near, the beat of the alarming drum
Roused up the soldier ere the morning star;
While thronged the citizens with terror dumb,
Or whispering, with white lips – The foe! They come! they
come!

Last noon beheld them full of lusty life,
Last eve in Beauty's circle proudly gay,
The midnight brought the signal-sound of strife,
The morn the marshalling in arms, – the day
Battle's magnificently-stern array!
The thunder-clouds close o'er it, which when rent
The earth is covered thick with other clay
Which her own clay shall cover, heaped and pent,
Rider and horse, – friend, foe, – in one red burial blent!

George Gordon, Lord Byron

After the failure of his Russian campaign in 1812, Napoleon had abdicated and had been sent into exile on the island of Elba. But in 1815 he contrived a brilliant return and his old soldiers flocked to rejoin him. The nations of Europe rallied in opposition and the two armies met at Waterloo in Belgium. It was a hard-fought battle, which the allied army under Wellington came close to losing on two occasions, but as the sun set at 8.15 the Duke gave the order for a general advance and won the day. Interestingly, although Waterloo tends to be acclaimed as a British victory, in an allied army of 67,000 men only 21,000 were in fact British.

THE 'CHORUS OF THE YEARS' SURVEYS THE FIELD OF WATERLOO BEFORE THE BATTLE

from **The Dynasts**

Yea, the coneys are scared by the thud of hoofs,
And their white scuts flash at their vanishing heels,
And swallows abandon the hamlet-roofs.

The mole's tunnelled chambers are crushed by wheels,
The lark's eggs scattered, their owners fled;
And the hedgehog's household the sapper unseals.

The snail draws in at the terrible tread,
But in vain; he is crushed by the felloe-rim;
The worm asks what can be overhead,

And wriggles deep from a scene so grim,
And guesses him safe; for he does not know
What a foul red flood will be soaking him!

Beaten about by the heel and toe
Are butterflies, sick of the day's long rheum,
To die of a worse than the weather-foe.

Trodden and bruised to a miry tomb
Are ears that have greened but will never be gold,
And flowers in the bud that will never bloom.

Thomas Hardy

1819

THE PETERLOO MASSACRE

With Henry Hunt We'll Go

With Henry Hunt we'll go, my boys,
With Henry Hunt we'll go;
We'll mount the cap of liberty
In spite of Nadin Joe.

'Twas on the sixteenth day of August,
Eighteen hundred and nineteen,
A meeting held in Peter Street
Was glorious to be seen;
Joe Nadin and his big bull-dogs,
Which you might plainly see,
And on the other side
Stood the bloody cavalry.

Anonymous

Orator Hunt was a radical reformer who advocated annual Parliaments and universal suffrage. He was billed to speak to a mass meeting at St Peter's Fields, Manchester, on 16 August 1819. Alarmed at the possibility of a general uprising, the authorities ordered the Manchester Yeomanry, which consisted largely of merchants, farmers and small tradesmen, to charge the mob that had gathered. In this famous engagement, known as the Peterloo Massacre, eleven people were killed. Hunt was arrested and imprisoned for two and a half years. This is the only surviving fragment of a popular song commemorating the event. Joe Nadin was the Deputy Constable of Manchester.

England in 1819

An old, mad, blind, despised, and dying king, –
Princes, the dregs of their dull race, who flow
Through public scorn, – mud from a muddy spring, –
Rulers who neither see, nor feel, nor know,
But leech-like to their fainting country cling,
Till they drop, blind in blood, without a blow, –
A people starved and stabbed in the untilled field, –
An army, which liberticide and prey
Makes as a two-edged sword to all who wield, –
Golden and sanguine laws which tempt and slay;
Religion Christless, Godless – a book sealed;
A Senate, – Time's worst statute unrepealed, –
Are graves, from which a glorious Phantom may
Burst, to illumine our tempestuous day.

Percy Bysshe Shelley

King George IV, 1820–30

1820

THE PRINCE REGENT

from The Political House that Jack Built

This is THE MAN – all shaven and shorn,
All cover'd with Orders – and all forlorn;
THE DANDY OF SIXTY, who bows with a grace,
And has *taste* in wigs, collars, cuirasses and lace;
Who, to tricksters, and fools, leaves the State and its treasure,
And, when Britain's in tears, sails about at his pleasure;
Who spurn'd from his presence the Friends of his youth,
And now has not one who will tell him the truth;
Who took to his counsels, in evil hour,
The Friends to the Reasons of lawless Power;
That back the Public Informer, who
Would put down the *Thing*, that, in spite of new Acts,
And attempts to restrain it, by Soldiers of Tax,
Will *poison* the Vermin,
That plunder the Wealth,
That lay in the House,
That Jack built.

William Hone

William Hone started out as a bookseller, but went on to become a
radical publisher. In 1820 he issued what was to be the most popular
satirical pamphlet of the nineteenth century, 'The Political House that
Jack Built', illustrated by George Cruikshank, who later achieved fame
with his illustrations for *Oliver Twist*. Hone's pamphlet satirized many
famous people, and within a year it had run into fifty-two editions.

QUEEN CAROLINE

The Bath

The weather's hot – the cabin's free!
  And she's as free and hot as either!
And Berghy is as hot as she!
  In short, they all are hot together!
Bring then a large capacious tub,
  And pour great pails of water in,
In which the frowzy nymph may rub
  The itchings of her royal skin.

Let none but Berghy's hand untie
  The garter, or unlace the boddice;
Let none but Berghy's faithful eye
  Survey the beauties of the goddess.

While *she* receives the copious shower
  He gets a step in honour's path,
And grows from this auspicious hour
  A K-night Companion of the Bath.
                    William Hone

George had married Caroline in 1795 and, after the birth of a daughter, Charlotte, they separated. When he became Regent in 1811, Caroline went to live on the Continent, accompanied by her major-domo, Bartolomeo Bergami, who served, it was said, all her needs. In 1820, on George's accession, she returned, and the luckless Prime Minister, Lord Liverpool, had to move a Bill dissolving the marriage and depriving her of the title of Queen. Her case was taken up by the Whigs and she became as popular as her husband was unpopular. The Bill was dropped, but she was refused entry to Westminster Abbey at the Coronation and died suddenly later in the year. Max Beerbohm said of Caroline that she had been cast for a tragic role, but played it in tights.

On the Queen

Most Gracious Queen, we thee implore
To go away and sin no more,
But if that effort be too great,
To go away at any rate.

Anonymous

1825

THE FOUNDATION OF LONDON UNIVERSITY

from **The London University**

Ye Dons and ye doctors, ye Provosts and Proctors,
   Who'rer paid to monopolize knowledge,
Come make opposition by voice and petition
   To the radical infidel College;
Come put forth your powers in aid of the towers
   Which boast of their Bishops and Martyrs,
And arm all the terrors of privileged errors
   Which live by the wax of their Charters.

Let Mackintosh battle with Canning and Vattel,
   Let Brougham be a friend to the 'niggers,'
Burdett cure the nation's misrepresentations,
   And Hume cut a figure in figures;
But let them not babble of Greek to the rabble.
   Nor teach the mechanics their letters;
The labouring classes were born to be asses,
   And not to be aping their betters.

'Tis a terrible crisis for Cam and for Isis!
   Fat butchers are learning dissection;
And looking-glass makers become Sabbath-breakers
   To study the rules of reflection;
'Sin: ϕ' and 'sin: θ' what sins can be sweeter?
   Are taught to the poor of both sexes,

And weavers and spinners jump up from their dinners
    To flirt with their Y's and their X's.

Chuckfarthing advances the doctrine of chances
    In spite of the staff of the beadle;
And menders of breeches between the long stitches
    Write books on the laws of the needle;
And chandlers all chatter of luminous matter,
    Who communicate none to their tallows,
And rogues get a notion of the pendulum's motion
    Which is only of use at the gallows.

Winthrop Mackworth Praed

Until 1825 there had been four universities in Scotland, but only two in England: Oxford and Cambridge; and these excluded Jews, Catholics and Dissenters. The Scottish poet Thomas Campbell and Henry Brougham, a prickly politician – who was later to retire to France and make Cannes a fashionable resort – decided to establish a new university in London, with no clergy on its governing body. They sold shares in it, and representatives of the great liberal families subscribed – J. S. Mill, Macaulay and Goldsmid among them. They founded University College in Gower Street. There, towards the end of the century, J. A. Fleming invented the thermionic valve, without which the wireless, television and computer could not have been developed.

A RETROSPECT

George the First was always reckoned
Vile, but viler George the Second;
And what mortal ever heard
Any good of George the Third?
When from earth the Fourth descended
(God be praised!) the Georges ended.

Walter Savage Landor

King William IV, 1830–7

1832

THE REFORM BILL

from **Pledges, by a Ten-Pound Householder**

When a gentleman comes
With his trumpet and drums,
And hangs out a flag at the Dragon,
    Some pledges, no doubt,
    We must get him to spout
To the shopkeepers, out of a wagon.

For although an MP
May be wiser than we
Till the House is dissolved, in December,
    Thenceforth, we're assured,
    Since Reform is secured,
We'll be wiser by far than our member.

A pledge must be had
That, since times are so bad
He'll prepare a long speech, to improve them;
    And since taxes, at best,
    Are a very poor jest,
He'll take infinite pains to remove them.

He must solemnly say
That he'll vote no more pay
To the troops, in their ugly red jackets;
    And that none may complain
    On the banks of the Seine,
He'll dismast all our ships, but the packets.

That the labourer's arm,
May be stout on the farm,
That our commerce may wake from stagnation,

That our trades may revive,
    And our looms look alive,
He'll be pledged to all free importation.

We must bind him, poor man,
    To obey their divan
However their worships may task him,
    To swallow their lies
    Without any surprise,
And to vote black is white, when they ask him.

These hints I shall lay,
    In a forcible way,
Before an intelligent quorum,
    Who meet to debate
    Upon matters of State,
Tonight, at the National Forum

Winthrop Mackworth Praed

In 1830 the Tory Government under Wellington was defeated at the polls and a coalition of Whigs, Liberals and Independents, led by the seventy-year-old Earl Grey, took office. Several future PMs – Lord John Russell, Melbourne and Palmerston – were in the Cabinet, and they were determined to bring in a Reform Bill that would abolish the rotten boroughs and widen the franchise to the extent of giving the vote to any male who occupied a house with a rental value of ten pounds or more. There was initial resistance in the Lords, but the Tories were badly led by Wellington and eventually the Bill was forced through. The measure itself had limited scope, being mainly a reform instituted by the middle classes on behalf of the middle classes, but the electorate was increased from 435,000 to 685,000. Revolution was avoided by a classic compromise, and England was set upon a path which was to lead to universal suffrage.

1834

THE TOLPUDDLE MARTYRS

God is our guide! from field, from wave,
From plough, from anvil, and from loom;
We come, our country's rights to save,

And speak a tyrant faction's doom:
We raise the watchword liberty;
We will, we will, we will be free!

God is our guide! no swords we draw,
We kindle not war's battle fires;
By reason, union, justice, law,
We claim the birthright of our sires:
We raise the watchword liberty;
We will, we will, we will be free!!!

George Loveless

George Loveless was the leader of a group of Dorsetshire labourers (the Tolpuddle Martyrs) who had 'combined together' to protect their jobs and their pay. This was an illegal act and the offenders were sentenced to seven years' deportation. After two years of protest, however, they were reprieved and Loveless returned to join the Chartists. He scribbled this poem on a piece of paper as his sentence was passed. He wrote: 'While we were being guarded back to prison, our hands being locked together, I tossed the above lines to some people that we passed; the guard, however, seizing hold of them, they were instantly carried back to the judge; and by some this was considered a crime of no less magnitude than high treason.' Tolpuddle has become the shrine of the Trade Union movement.

1835–41

MELBOURNE'S PREMIERSHIP

To promise, pause, prepare, postpone
And end by letting things alone:
In short, to earn the people's pay
By doing nothing every day.
Winthrop Mackworth Praed

Lord Melbourne told his secretary that being Prime Minister was 'a damned bore'. But he held the office for almost seven years and left it reluctantly in 1841. His behaviour was certainly laid-back, but the march of progress went on: local government was established, the Poor Law was introduced and the first factory acts were passed. From 1837 Melbourne relished the role of guide and mentor to the young Queen Victoria, who was convinced as a result that Whigs were good and Tories bad.

The Victorian Age, 1837–1901

Victoria succeeded to the throne in 1837 because her uncles, the sons of George III, did not produce any legitimate children. The new queen was a small woman, less than five feet tall, but she had the strength to bear nine children. In 1840 she had married one of her cousins, Albert of Saxe-Coburg, and for the first time in two hundred years the English monarchy enjoyed domestic bliss. Victoria imposed respectability upon the whole nation – middle-class morality displaced the rakishness of Regency England and parlour songs became the order of the day.

The nineteenth century was the high watermark of parliamentary democracy. The numbers allowed to vote increased until all men, though not women, had the vote in the 'Mother of Parliaments'. Political debates were widely reported and read, and the great prime ministers, Robert Peel, Disraeli and Gladstone, all became popular figures.

The power of Britain seemed unassailable and through its Empire and colonies it became the policeman of the world. Apart from the Crimean War in the 1850s, in which Britain suffered its most glorious defeat in the Charge of the Light Brigade, the British Army did not fight in Europe. It was spread throughout the Empire and engaged in a number of little wars in China, India, Afghanistan, Zululand, the Sudan, Egypt and West Africa. The British 'Tommy' held the Empire together. Of the 100,000 enlisted men, three-quarters served overseas.

It was a period of great prosperity and British goods, engines and ships made in Lancashire, Yorkshire, Glasgow and Birmingham flooded the world. Alongside the vast wealth there was also great poverty. The condition of the poor became increasingly a political issue and a problem that had to be addressed. Towards the end of the century, the politics of Ireland consumed all the political parties and leading figures, as various solutions to the 'Irish Problem' were tried and failed.

English literature flourished – the novels of Charles Dickens, George Eliot, William Makepeace Thackeray and Anthony Trollope were read by millions. The poet Robert Browning became famous through his elopement to Italy and the Poet Laureate, Alfred, Lord Tennyson, was made a peer.

Queen Victoria, 1837–1901

PRINCE ALBERT

I am a German just arrived,
    With you for to be mingling,
My passage it was paid,
    From Germany to England;
To wed your blooming Queen.
    For better or worse I take her,
My father is a duke,
    And I'm a sausage maker.

Here I am in rags and jags,
    Come from the land of all dirt,
I married England's Queen.
    My name it is young Albert.

I am a cousin to the Queen,
    And our mothers they are cronies,
My father lives at home,
    And deals in nice polonies:
Lots of sour crout and broom,
    For money he'll be giving,
And by working very hard,
    He gets a tidy living.

Here I am, &c.

She says now we are wed.
    I must not dare to tease her,
But strive both day and night,
    All e'er I can to please her,
I told her I would do
    For her all I was able,
And when she had a son
    I would sit and rock the cradle.

Here I am, &c.

Anonymous

Victoria was the only child of the fourth son of George III, the Duke of Kent, who died a few months after her birth. None of George's other older sons produced legitimate children and so she succeeded by default.

Victoria was brought up by her German mother, and she was not allowed to mix with children of her own age. Her mother tried to dominate and influence her daughter but, when Victoria became Queen at the age of eighteen, the duchess was pushed into the background. Her first language was German and she always spoke English with a guttural accent. Victoria's accession saved the monarchy.

Three years later she married her cousin, Prince Albert of Saxe-Coburg, who had been groomed to become her consort. She became a devoted wife. The ballad-mongers in London had much fun at Albert's expense, emphasizing his German origins and the fact that he had no money. But Albert soon became very anglicized.

1838

Grace Darling

After you had steered your coble out of the storm
And left the smaller islands to break the surface,
Like draughts shaking that colossal backcloth there came
Fifty pounds from the Queen, proposals of marriage.

The daughter of a lighthouse-keeper and the saints
Who once lived there on birds' eggs, rainwater, barley
And built to keep all pilgrims at a safe distance
Circular houses with views only of the sky,

Who set timber burning on the top of a tower
Before each was launched at last in his stone coffin –
You would turn your back on mainland and suitor
To marry, then bereave the waves from Lindisfarne,

A moth against the lamp that shines still and reveals
Many small boats at sea, lifeboats, named after girls.
Michael Longley

When the steamer *Forfarshire* ran aground off the Farne rocks in September 1838, Grace Darling, the twenty-two-year-old daughter of the lighthouse keeper, rowed out with her father in a great storm and helped him save nine people from the wreck. She became an instant heroine: souvenir mugs were produced and admirers offered £5 for a lock of her hair. She continued to live with her father until her death from tuberculosis just four years later. There is a marble effigy of her in Bamburgh churchyard, complete with an oar in her right hand and seaweed carved on the canopy.

1841

THE BIRTH OF EDWARD, PRINCE OF WALES

There's a pretty fuss and bother both in country and in town,
Since we have got a present, and an heir unto the Crown,
A little Prince of Wales so charming and so sly,
And the ladies shout with wonder, What a pretty little boy!

He must have a little musket, a trumpet and a kite,
A little penny rattle, and silver sword so bright,
A little cap and feather with scarlet coat so smart,
And a pretty little hobby horse to ride about the park.

He must have a dandy suit to strut about the town,
John Bull must rake together six or seven thousand pound,
You'd laugh to see his daddy, at night he homeward runs,
With some peppermint or lollipops, sweet cakes and sugar plums.

Now to get these little niceties the taxes must be rose,
For the little Prince of Wales wants so many suits of clothes,
So they must tax the frying pan, the windows and the doors,
The bedsteads and the tables, kitchen pokers, and the floors.

John Harkness

The Prince had to wait sixty years before ascending the throne as Edward VII, but seems never to have lost his taste for idle and expensive pleasures.

1846

THE REPEAL OF THE CORN LAWS

from **Corn Law Rhymes**

Child, is thy father dead?
  Father is gone!
Why did they tax his bread?
  God's will be done!
Mother has sold her bed;
Better to die than wed!
Where shall she lay her head?
  Home we have none!

Father clamm'd thrice a week –
  God's will be done!
Long for work did he seek,
  Work he found none.
Tears on his hollow cheek
Told what no tongue could speak:
Why did his master break?
  God's will be done!

Doctor said air was best –
  Food we had none;
Father, with panting breast,
  Groan'd to be gone:
Now he is with the blest –
Mother says death is best!
We have no place of rest –
  Yes, ye have one!

Ebenezer Elliott

The big issue of the 1840s was whether the Corn Laws, which protected British farmers, should be repealed to allow for cheaper foreign imports. The Anti Corn Law League, which was formed in 1839 and led by John Bright and Richard Cobden, campaigned vigorously across the country. Prime Minister Sir Robert Peel had become a convert to free trade, through learning of the failure of the Irish potato crop and of the prospect of famine. In 1846 he repealed the Corn Laws, lost office and split the Tory party. Two hundred and thirty-one Tory MPs voted against him. The old party of Pitt, Canning, Liverpool and Wellington broke up. The issue – free trade as against protection – was the same that divided the Tories in 1906, and in both instances disunity was to lead to long periods of government by the opposition.

1848

THE RAILWAYS

'Mr Dombey', *from* Victorian Trains

The whistle blows. The train moves.
Thank God I am pulling away from the conversation
I had on the platform through the hissing of steam
With that man who dares to wear crape for the death of my son.
But I forget. He is coming with us.
He is always ahead of us stocking the engine.
I depend on him to convey me
With my food and my drink and my wraps and my reading material
To my first holiday since grief mastered me.
He is the one with the view in front of him
The ash in his whiskers, the speed in his hair.

He is richer now. He refused my tip.
Death and money roll round and round
In my head with the wheels.
I know what a skeleton looks like.
I never think of my dead son
In this connection. I think of wealth.

The railway is like a skeleton,
Alive in a prosperous body,
Reaching up to grasp Yorkshire and Lancashire
Kicking Devon and Kent
Squatting on London.

A diagram of growth
A midwinter leaf.

I am a merchant
With fantasies like all merchants.
Gold, carpets, handsome women come to me
Out of the sea, along these tracks.
I am as rich as England,
As solid as a town hall.

Patricia Beer

The first railway line, running between Stockton and Darlington, was
opened in 1825, and the 1830s saw a modest expansion, until by 1838
there were more than 500 miles of track, with London and Birmingham
included in the service. The railway boom, whose driving force was
George Hudson, the 'Railway King', took off in the 1840s, but burst in
1847, by which time more than 5,000 miles of track had been laid and
English industry and society had been transformed. Dickens published
Dombey and Son in 1848, and the railways play an important part in the
book. To Mr Dombey, the cold, proud and stubborn merchant, they
represent progress. His sickly son, Paul, has a foster-mother, Polly
Toodle, whose husband is a stoker and engine-driver. But Paul is
removed from their care and submitted to a wretched and loveless
education, and many Victorians wept over his early death.

1851

THE GREAT EXHIBITION

Fountains, gushing silver light,
  Sculptures, soft and warm and fair,
Gems, that bind the dazzled sight,
  Silken trophies rich and rare,
Wondrous works of cunning skill,
  Precious miracles of art, –
How your crowding memories fill
  Mournfully my musing heart!

Fairy Giant choicest birth
  Of the Beautiful Sublime,
Seeming like the Toy of earth
  Given to the dotard Time, –
Glacier-diamond, Alp of glass,
  Sindbad's cave, Aladdin's hall, –
Must it then be crush'd, alas;
  Must the Crystal Palace fall?

Anonymous

Prince Albert organized the Great Exhibition to celebrate Britain's industrial and commercial leadership of the world. It was housed in an enormous structure of glass and steel, the Crystal Palace, which was erected in Hyde Park and later moved to South London. Disraeli, never at a loss for hyperbole, hailed it as 'an enchanted pile, which the sagacious taste and prescient philanthropy of an accomplished and enlightened Prince have raised for the glory of England and the instruction of two hemispheres'.

The Great Exhibition made a profit and on the strength of this, land was bought in South Kensington for Imperial College and the museums that now stand there. The Crystal Palace itself was moved to Sydenham, where it proved a costly embarrassment until it was burnt down in the next century.

1852

THE DEATH OF WELLINGTON

from **Ode on the Death of the Duke of Wellington**

Bury the Great Duke
   With an empire's lamentation,
Let us bury the Great Duke
   To the noise of the mourning of a mighty nation,
Mourning when their leaders fall,
Warriors carry the warrior's pall,
And sorrow darkens hamlet and hall.

Lead out the pageant: sad and slow,
As fits an universal woe,
Let the long long procession go,
And let the sorrowing crowd about it grow,
And let the mournful martial music blow;
The last great Englishman is low . . .
                    Alfred, Lord Tennyson

from **Don Juan**

You are 'the best of cut-throats:' – do not start;
   The phrase is Shakespeare's, and not misapplied: –
War's a brain-spattering, windpipe-slitting art,
   Unless her cause by right be sanctified.
If you have acted *once* a generous part,
   The world, not the world's masters, will decide,
And I shall be delighted to learn who,
Save you and yours, have gain'd by Waterloo?

I am no flatterer – you've supp'd full of flattery:
   They say you like it too – 't is no great wonder.
He whose whole life has been assault and battery,
   At last may get a little tired of thunder;
And swallowing eulogy much more than satire, he

May like being praised for every lucky blunder,
Call'd 'Saviour of the Nations' – not yet saved,
And 'Europe's Liberator' – still enslaved.

George Gordon, Lord Byron

When he died, Wellington was given a splendid state funeral, as befitted a national hero. Writing forty years earlier, Byron evidently did not share the general adulation, but it is unlikely that Wellington, who once replied to a blackmailing courtesan with the words, 'Publish and be damned!' lost much sleep over this.

THE WEAVING INDUSTRY

from **The Hand-Loom Weavers' Lament**

You gentlemen and tradesmen, that ride about at will,
Look down on these poor people; it's enough to make you crill;
Look down on these poor people, as you ride up and down,
I think there is a God above will bring your pride quite down.
    You tyrants of England, your race may soon be run,
    You may be brought unto account for what you've sorely
done.

You pull down our wages, shamefully to tell;
You go into the markets, and say you cannot sell;
And when that we do ask you when these bad times will mend,
You quickly give an answer, 'When the wars are at an end.'
    You tyrants of England, &c.

Anonymous

The weaving industry was essentially a cottage industry, providing work not only for the weavers but for all the ancillary trades of shearing, wool-cropping and sorting, combing, spinning, bleaching, dyeing, and making up garments. The weekly wages of hand-loom weavers fell from 27 shillings in 1814 to 6 shillings in 1832. This destroyed the hand-loom cottage industry and weavers had no option but to work in factories.

1853

A PUBLIC HANGING

A London Fête

All night fell hammers, shock on shock;
With echoes Newgate's granite clanged:
The scaffold built, at eight o'clock
They brought the man out to be hanged.
Then came from all the people there
A single cry, that shook the air;
Mothers held up their babes to see,
Who spread their hands, and crowed for glee;
Here a girl from her vesture tore
A rag to wave with, and joined the roar;
There a man, with yelling tired,
Stopped, and the culprit's crime inquired;
A sot, below the doomed man dumb,
Bawled his health in the world to come;
These blasphemed and fought for places;
Those half-crushed, cast frantic faces,
To windows, where, in freedom sweet,
Others enjoyed the wicked treat.
At last, the show's black crisis pended;
Struggles for better standings ended;
The rabble's lips no longer cursed,
But stood agape with horrid thirst;
Thousands of breasts beat horrid hope;
Thousands of eyeballs, lit with hell,
Burnt one way all, to see the rope
Unslacken as the platform fell.
The rope flew tight; and then the roar
Burst forth afresh; less loud, but more
Confused and affrighting than before.
A few harsh tongues for ever led
The common din, the chaos of noises,
But ear could not catch what they said.
As when the realm of the damned rejoices

At winning a soul to its will,
That clatter and clangour of hateful voices
Sickened and stunned the air, until
The dangling corpse hung straight and still.
The show complete, the pleasure past,
The solid masses loosened fast:
A thief slunk off, with ample spoil,
To ply elsewhere his daily toil;
A baby strung its doll to a stick;
A mother praised the pretty trick;
Two children caught and hanged a cat;
Two friends walked on, in lively chat;
And two, who had disputed places,
Went forth to fight, with murderous faces.
       Coventry Patmore

Public executions were not stopped in England until 1868. Thackeray in
1840, and Dickens in a famous letter to *The Times* in 1849, had both tried
to bring them to an end. Coventry Patmore denied in later years that he
had attacked the imposition of the death penalty, but the last couplet of
this poem effectively demolishes the deterrent argument.

1854

The Charge of the Light Brigade

Half a league, half a league,
 Half a league onward,
All in the valley of Death
 Rode the six hundred.
'Forward, the Light Brigade!
Charge for the guns!' he said:
Into the valley of Death
 Rode the six hundred.

'Forward, the Light Brigade!'
Was there a man dismayed?
Not though the soldier knew
 Someone had blundered:

Their's not to make reply,
Their's not to reason why,
Their's but to do and die:
Into the valley of Death
  Rode the six hundred.

Cannon to right of them,
Cannon to left of them,
Cannon behind them
  Volleyed and thundered;
Stormed at with shot and shell,
Boldly they rode and well,
Into the jaws of Death,
Into the mouth of Hell
  Rode the six hundred.

Flashed all their sabres bare,
Flashed as they turned in air
Sabring the gunners there,
Charging an army, while
  All the world wondered:

Plunged in the battery-smoke
Right through the line they broke;
Cossack and Russian
Reeled from the sabre-stroke
  Shattered and sundered.
Then they rode back, but not
  Not the six hundred.

Cannon to right of them,
Cannon to left of them,
Cannon behind of them
  Volleyed and thundered;
Stormed at with shot and shell,
While horse and hero fell,
They that had fought so well
Came through the jaws of Death,
Back from the mouth of Hell,
All that was left of them,
  Left of six hundred.

When can their glory fade?
O the wild charge they made!
   All the world wondered.
Honour the charge they made!
Honour the Light Brigade,
   Noble six hundred!
          Alfred, Lord Tennyson

The Crimean War had started in 1854 to prevent Russia from seizing parts of the crumbling Turkish Empire. War fever swept the country, but the British army itself was in a ramshackle state. The soldier's pay of a shilling a day came down, after deductions, to no more than three pence; commissions were for sale; and the organization of supplies and medical care were both scandalously bad. Lord Raglan, the Commander-in-Chief, had not seen service for twenty-five years, and Lord Cardigan, who led the Light Brigade, was a buffoon. Between them they brought about one of the most memorable failures in the history of the British army. The war ended in 1856, and Russia's ambitions had been contained at the cost of 25,000 British dead.

Florence Nightingale

Through your pocket glass you have let disease expand
To remote continents of pain where you go far
With rustling cuff and starched apron, a soft hand:
Beneath the bandage maggots are stitching the scar.

For many of the men who lie there it is late
And you allow them at the edge of consciousness
The halo of our lamp, a brothel's fanlight
Or a nightlight carried in by nanny and nurse.

You know that even with officers and clergy
Moustachioed lips will purse into fundaments
And under sedation all the bad words emerge
To be rinsed in your head like the smell of wounds,

Death's vegetable sweetness at both rind and core –
Name a weed and you find it growing everywhere.
          Michael Longley

In 1854 Florence Nightingale was thirty-five years old, a trained nurse and a friend of the War Minister, Sydney Herbert. Incensed by reports in *The Times* of the way in which soldiers wounded in the Crimean War were being treated, she took it upon herself to lead a small group of volunteer nurses to Scutari, the British military hospital base in Constantinople. The conditions she found there, just ten days after the battle of Balaclava, were appalling. Rats, maggots and lice overran the wards; twenty chamber-pots were shared between 2,000 men; and amid all that filth and indifference typhus, cholera, dysentery, delirium and death flourished. With tremendous vitality and drive she set about cleaning the place up. As she went round the wards with her lamp, wounded soldiers would kiss her passing shadow. Her conduct brought her enemies, principally among the doctors, and when the chief medical officer was awarded the KCB she suggested that it stood for 'Knight of the Crimea Burial-ground'.

On returning to England, she was warmly supported by the Queen and over the next fifty years she became the second most famous woman in the country. By establishing the Nightingale School for Nurses at St Thomas's, she laid the foundations of modern nursing. She lived on until 1907 – a one-woman powerhouse, a relentless reformer and a legend. Characteristically, she once wrote: 'From committees, charity and schism – from the Church of England and all other deadly sins – from philanthropy and all the deceits of the devil – Good Lord deliver us.'

VICTORIANA

Mr Gradgrind's Country

There was a dining-room, there was a drawing-room,
There was a billiard-room, there was a morning-room,
There were bedrooms for guests and bedrooms for sons and daughters,
In attic and basement there were ample servants' quarters,
There was a modern bathroom, a strong-room, and a conservatory.
In the days of England's glory.

There were Turkish carpets, there were Axminster carpets,
There were oil paintings of Vesuvius and family portraits,
There were mirrors, ottomans, wash-hand-stands and tantaluses,
There were port, sherry, claret, liqueur, and champagne glasses,
There was a solid brass gong, a grand piano, antlers, decanters, and a gentlemen's lavatory,
In the days of England's glory.

There was marqueterie and there was mahogany,
There was a cast of the Dying Gladiator in his agony,
There was the 'Encyclopaedia Britannica' in a revolving bookcase,
There were finger-bowls, asparagus-tongs, and inlets of real lace:
They stood in their own grounds and were called Chatsworth, Elgin, or Tobermory,
In the days of England's glory.

But now these substantial gentlemen's establishments
Are like a perspective of disused elephants,
And the current Rajahs of industry flash past their wide frontages
Far far away to the latest things in labour-saving cottages,
Where with Russell lupins, jade ash-trays, some Sealyham terriers, and a migratory
Cook they continue the story.

Sylvia Townsend Warner

Dickens's *Hard Times* appeared in 1854. Mr Gradgrind is one of its characters: a tyrannical patriarch whose views on education are limited to a belief in stuffing children's heads with facts.

FACTORY CONDITIONS

from **The Cry of the Children**

Do you hear the children weeping, O my brothers,
    Ere the sorrow comes with years?
They are leaning their young heads against their mothers, –
    And *that* cannot stop their tears.
The young lambs are bleating in the meadows;
   The young birds are chirping in the nest;
The young fawns are playing with the shadows;
   The young flowers are blowing toward the west –
But the young, young children, O my brothers,
    They are weeping bitterly –
They are weeping in the playtime of the others,
    In the country of the free.

'For oh,' say the children, 'we are weary,
    And we cannot run or leap –
If we cared for any meadows, it were merely
    To drop down in them and sleep.
Our knees tremble sorely in the stooping –
   We fall upon our faces, trying to go;
And, underneath our heavy eyelids drooping,
   The reddest flower would look as pale as snow.
For, all day, we drag our burden tiring,
    Through the coal-dark, underground –
Or, all day, we drive the wheels of iron.
    In the factories, round and round.

'For, all day, the wheels are droning, turning, –
    Their wind comes in our faces, –
Till our hearts turn, – our head, with pulses burning,
    And the walls turn in their places –
Turns the sky in the high window blank and reeling –

Turns the long light that droppeth down the wall –
Turn the black flies that crawl along the ceiling –
    All are turning, all the day, and we with all –
And all day, the iron wheels are droning;
    And sometimes we could pray,
"O ye wheels," (breaking out in a mad moaning)
    "Stop! be silent for today!" '

They look up, with their pale and sunken faces,
    And their look is dread to see,
For they mind you of their angels in their places,
    With eyes meant for Deity; –
'How long,' they say, 'how long, O cruel nation,
    Will you stand, to move the world, on a child's heart, –
Stifle down with a mail'd heel its palpitation,
    And tread onward to your throne amid the mart?
Our blood splashes upward, O our tyrants,
    And your purple shows your path;
But the child's sob curseth deeper in the silence
    Than the strong man in his wrath!'

Elizabeth Barrett Browning

In most factories conditions were appalling. In 1830 a Tory churchman, Richard Oastler, had started a crusade in Yorkshire against child slavery. In 1834 a law was passed forbidding children under the age of nine to be put to work, while those under thirteen were restricted to a

nine-hour day, and those between fourteen and eighteen to a twelve-hour day. Dickens wrote of the misery he endured as a young boy employed in a blacking factory. Young girls worked in pits, drawing the wagons. Later, Lord Shaftesbury took up the cause of reform, and in 1850 a maximum ten-and-a-half-hour working day was agreed upon, with seven and a half hours on Saturdays. In 1876 Disraeli fixed a fifty-six-hour week and the Trade Unions were released from criminal liability. Shaftesbury is commemorated by the statue of Eros in Piccadilly Circus – a strange tribute in a strange place for such a good man.

1861

VICTORIA WITHOUT ALBERT

The Widow at Windsor

'Ave you 'eard o' the Widow at Windsor
  With a hairy gold crown on 'er 'ead?
She 'as ships on the foam – she 'as millions at 'ome,
  An' she pays us poor beggars in red.
    (Ow, poor beggars in red!)
There's 'er nick on the cavalry 'orses,
  There's 'er mark on the medical stores –
An' 'er troopers you'll find with a fair wind be'ind
  That takes us to various wars.
      (Poor beggars – barbarious wars!)
        Then 'ere's to the Widow at Windsor,
          An' 'ere's to the stores an' the guns,
        The men an' the 'orses what makes up the forces
          O' Missis Victorier's sons.
          (Poor beggars! Victorier's sons!)

Walk wide o' the Widow at Windsor,
  For 'alf o' Creation she owns:
We 'ave bought 'er the same with the sword an' the flame,
  An' we've salted it down with our bones.
    (Poor beggars – it's blue with our bones!)
Hands off o' the Sons o' the Widow,

Hands off o' the goods in 'er shop,
For the Kings must come down an' the Emperors frown
When the Widow at Windsor says 'Stop!'
    (Poor beggars – we're sent to say 'Stop!')
        Then 'ere's to the Lodge o' the Widow,
            From the Pole to the Tropics it runs –
        To the Lodge that we tile with the rank an' the file,
            An' open in form with the guns.
        (Poor beggars! – it's always they guns!)

We 'ave 'eard o' the Widow at Windsor,
    It's safest to leave 'er alone:
For 'er sentries we stand by the sea an' the land
    Wherever the bugles are blown.
        (Poor beggars! – an' don't we get blown!)
Take 'old o' the Wings o' the Mornin',
    An' flop round the earth till you're dead;
But you won't get away from the tune that they play
    To the bloomin' old rag over'ead.
        (Poor beggars – it's 'ot over'ead!)
            Then 'ere's to the Sons of the Widow,
                Wherever, 'owever they roam.
            'Ere's all they desire, an' if they require
                A speedy return to their 'ome.
            (Poor beggars – they'll never see 'ome!)
                                    Rudyard Kipling

After the death of Albert in 1861 from dysentery caught from the bad drains at Windsor Castle, Victoria entered a prolonged period of mourning. This withdrawal made her a remote and rather unpopular figure. Prime Minister Benjamin Disraeli coaxed her out of retirement, however, and she continued to reign until 1901. This poem is supposed to have cost Kipling any sign of royal favour during the Queen's lifetime. She was not amused.

1878

TURKEY AND JINGOISM

We don't want to fight, but, by Jingo, if we do,
We've got the ships, we've got the men, we've got the money too.
We've fought the Bear before, and, while Britons shall be true,
    The Russians shall not have Constantinople.

G. W. Hunt

In 1877 Russia declared war on Turkey with a view to seizing as much of Turkey's Balkan Empire as it could. Popular feeling in Britain was for the Turks, in spite of the savage massacre they had inflicted upon the Bulgarians in 1876, and a wave of militarism swept the country. The topical musical-hall song from which the refrain above is taken led to the coining of a new word, 'jingoism'. Disraeli ordered the fleet to sail to Constantinople, the reserves were called up and Indian troops were moved to the Mediterranean. The last thing Disraeli wanted was a war, but Russia's ambitions had to be checked, especially as its lands bordered on India. Heads of state gathered at the Congress of Berlin, and there, through his diplomacy, Disraeli secured 'peace with honour'.

Vitaï Lampada

There's a breathless hush in the Close to-night –
    Ten to make and the match to win –
A bumping pitch and a blinding light,
    An hour to play and the last man in.
And it's not for the sake of a ribboned coat,
    Or the selfish hope of a season's fame,
But his Captain's hand on his shoulder smote –
    'Play up! play up! and play the game!'

The sand of the desert is sodden red, –
    Red with the wreck of a square that broke; –
The Gatling's jammed and the Colonel dead,
    And the regiment blind with dust and smoke.

The river of death has brimmed his banks,
    And England's far, and Honour a name,
But the voice of a schoolboy rallies the ranks:
    'Play up! play up! and play the game!'

This is the word that year by year,
    While in her place the School is set,
Every one of her sons must hear,
    And none that hears it dare forget.
This they all with a joyful mind
    Bear through life like a torch in flame,
And falling fling to the host behind –
    'Play up! play up! and play the game!'

                                            Henry Newbolt

Newbolt was one of the leading poets of British Imperialism. To him
the individual was all and generations of schoolboys read this poem as
it embodied the spirit of fearless optimism and personal gallantry.
Leadership and spirit were needed but Belloc was closer to the mark on
the power of imperialism when he said, 'What matters is that we have
got the Maxim gun and they have not.' This romantic dream was finally
shattered in the First World War when the concept of individual
chivalry sank into the mud of Flanders.

1885

THE DEATH OF GENERAL GORDON

from **The Hero of Khartoum**

Alas! now o'er the civilized world there hangs a gloom
For brave General Gordon, that was killed in Khartoum;
He was a Christian hero, and a soldier of the Cross,
And to England his death will be a very great loss.

He was very cool in temper, generous and brave,
The friend of the poor, the sick, and the slave;
And many a poor boy he did educate,
And laboured hard to do so early and late.

He always took the Bible for his guide,
And he liked little boys to walk by his side;
He preferred their company more so than men,
Because he knew there was less guile in them.

And in his conversation he was modest and plain,
Denouncing all pleasures he considered sinful and vain,
And in battle he carried no weapon but a small cane,
Whilst the bullets fell around him like a shower of rain.

In military life his equal couldn't be found,
No! if you were to search the wide world around,
And 'tis pitiful to think he has met with such a doom
By a base *traitor knave* while in Khartoum.

Yes, the black-hearted traitor opened the gates of Khartoum,
And through that the Christian hero has met his doom,
For when the gates were opened the Arabs rushed madly in,
And foully murdered him while they laughingly did grin.

William McGonagall

In 1882, at the instigation of the Prime Minister, William Ewart
Gladstone, Britain annexed Egypt with the intention of securing the
Suez Canal as the gateway to her Indian Empire. Three years later, a
Muslim leader, the Mahdi, raised a revolt in the Sudan, inflicting severe
losses on British troops. General Charles Gordon was sent by Gladstone

– The Grand Old Man, as he was called – to restore order, but found himself besieged at Khartoum. The Government in London was slow to respond, and when a relief force was sent, it arrived to find that Gordon had been killed two days earlier. The country and the Queen were outraged. Victoria sent an open telegram in which she deplored the 'frightful' delay and spoke of 'the stain left upon England'. Gladstone was called the Murderer of Gordon, and a topical poem went:

> The G.O.M., when his life ebbs out,
> Will ride in a fiery chariot,
>   And sit in state
>   On a red-hot plate
> Between Pilate and Judas Iscariot.

ASPECTS OF LATE VICTORIAN ENGLAND

1 THE NORTHERN TOWN

from Satan Absolved: a Victorian Mystery

> The smoke of their foul dens
> Broodeth on Thy Earth as a black pestilence,
> Hiding the kind day's eye. No flower, no grass there groweth,
> Only their engines' dung which the fierce furnace throweth.
> Their presence poisoneth all and maketh all unclean.
> Thy streams they have made sewers for their dyes analine.
> No fish therein may swim, no frog, no worm, may crawl,
> No snail for grime may build her house within their wall.
>
> *Wilfrid Scawen Blunt*

2 THE SUBURBS

from Thirty Bob a Week

> For like a mole I journey in the dark,
>   A-travelling along the underground
> From my Pillar'd Halls and broad Suburban Park,
>   To come the daily dull official round;
> And home again at night with my pipe all alight,
>   A-scheming how to count ten bob a pound.

And it's often very cold and very wet,
 And my missus stitches towels for a hunks;
And the Pillar'd Halls is half of it to let –
 Three rooms about the size of travelling trunks.
And we cough, my wife and I, to dislocate a sigh,
 When the noisy little kids are in their bunks.

But you never hear her do a growl or whine,
 For she's made of flint and roses, very odd;
And I've got to cut my meaning rather fine,
 Or I'd blubber, for I'm made of greens and sod:
So p'r'aps we are in Hell for all that I can tell,
 And lost and damn'd and serv'd up hot to God.
                                        John Davidson

3 THE COUNTRYSIDE

from **Why England is Conservative**

Let hound and horn in wintry woods and dells
Make jocund music though the boughs be bare,
And whistling yokel guide his teaming share
Hard by the homes where gentle lordship dwells.
Therefore sit high enthroned on every hill,
Authority! and loved in every vale;
Nor, old Tradition, falter in the tale
Of lowly valour led by lofty will;
And though the throats of envy rage and rail,
Be fair proud England, proud fair England still.
                                        Alfred Austin

In the nineteenth century, the pastoral society of eighteenth century England was transformed by the Industrial Revolution. The great cities and towns of the North grew rapidly – Manchester and Bolton were based on the cotton trade; Bradford, Leeds, and Huddersfield in Yorkshire were based on the woollen trade; and Birmingham and Coventry on engineering. These three poems describe aspects of that change. Rural life, of course, survived and to many became a dream of bliss, described romantically by Alfred Austin, who was the Poet Laureate and generally considered to be one of the worst occupants of

that post. The dark satanic mills turned the cities into thriving places of
activity but they also had congested, smoky and disease-ridden slums.
All around the cities, suburbs mushroomed. John Davidson, a Scot who
settled in London at the turn of the century, described what it was like
to live in a city and travel to work by underground train. Modern
Britain was taking shape.

1895

FIN DE SIÈCLE

The Arrest of Oscar Wilde at the Cadogan Hotel

He sipped at a weak hock and seltzer
　　As he gazed at the London skies
Through the Nottingham lace of the curtains
　　Or was it his bees-winged eyes?

To the right and before him Pont Street
　　Did tower in her new built red,
As hard as the morning gaslight
　　That shone on his unmade bed,

'I want some more hock in my seltzer,
　　And Robbie, please give me your hand –
Is this the end or beginning?
　　How can I understand?

'So you've brought me the latest *Yellow Book*:
　　And Buchan has got in it now:
Approval of what is approved of
　　Is as false as a well-kept vow.

'More hock, Robbie – where is the seltzer?
　　Dear boy, pull again at the bell!
They are all little better than *cretins*,
　　Though this *is* the Cadogan Hotel.

'One astrakhan coat is at Willis's –
　　Another one's at the Savoy:
Do fetch my morocco portmanteau,
　　And bring them on later, dear boy.'

A thump, and a murmur of voices –
 'Oh why must they make such a din?'
As the door of the bedroom swung open
 And TWO PLAIN CLOTHES POLICEMEN came in:

'Mr Woilde, we 'ave come for tew take yew
 Where felons and criminals dwell:
We must ask yew tew leave with us quoietly
 For this *is* the Cadogan Hotel.'

He rose, and he put down *The Yellow Book*.
 He staggered – and, terrible-eyed,
He brushed past the palms on the staircase
 And was helped to a hansom outside.

John Betjeman

In 1895 Oscar Wilde was the lion of London Society, the arbiter of taste and most celebrated of wits. His plays *The Ideal Husband* and *The Importance of Being Earnest* were being performed to packed houses. So brash and confident was he, that he openly flaunted his passionate affair with Lord Alfred Douglas, son of the Marquis of Queensberry. Incensed, the Marquis left a visiting card at Wilde's club addressed to 'Oscar Wilde posing as a Somdomite' – which was to prove a notorious misspelling. Wilde foolishly started a libel action and, in the course of a two-day cross-examination by Edward Carson, was disastrously compelled to admit that he had engaged in a number of casual homosexual affairs. He was advised to fly to France, but he went instead to the Cadogan Hotel in Sloane Street where he got slightly drunk with Douglas and his friend Robert Ross. Tried for practising 'the love that dare not speak its name', he was found guilty and sentenced to two years' hard labour. It was an appalling humiliation and Victorian society rejoiced in its revenge. From his time in prison, Wilde wrote his finest poem, 'The Ballad of Reading Gaol'. He died in poverty in France in 1900.

On reading Betjeman's poem, Lord Alfred Douglas complained that it was not very accurate.

1899–1902

The Boer War

The whip-crack of a Union Jack
In a stiff breeze (the ship will roll),
Deft abracadabra drums
Enchant the patriotic soul –

A grandsire in St James's Street
Sat at the window of his club,
His second son, shot through the throat,
Slid backwards down a slope of a scrub,

Gargled his last breaths, one by one by one,
In too much blood, too young to spill,
Died difficultly, drop by drop by drop –
'By your son's courage, sir, we took the hill.'

They took the hill (Whose hill? What for?)
But what a climb they left to do!
Out of that bungled, unwise war
An alp of unforgiveness grew.

William Plomer

In 1886, gold had been discovered in the Witwatersrand and the competition for South Africa started. There was a keen rivalry between the Boer settlers of Dutch descent and the British imperialists, lead by Cecil Rhodes. In 1899 the Government in London reluctantly decided to intervene to protect basic rights for the British. At first British troops met with a succession of humiliating defeats, but gradually, under the command of Lord Roberts, Kitchener and Baden-Powell, they successfully fought back. The cost, however, was enormous – 20,000 dead – and the greatest imperial power of the day had had to use 200,000 men to fight a mere 60,000 farmers. The Union of South Africa was the immediate result, but the end of the Empire had also moved a step closer.

Following British Failures Exposed by the Boer War

And ye vaunted your fathomless powers, and ye flaunted your
    iron pride,
Ere – ye fawned on the Younger Nations for the men who could
    shoot and ride!
Then ye returned to your trinkets; then ye contented your souls
With the flannelled fools at the wicket or the muddied oafs at
    the goals.

Rudyard Kipling

1901

THE DEATH OF QUEEN VICTORIA

from 1901

When Queen Victoria died
The whole of England mourned
Not for a so recently breathing old woman
A wife and a mother and a widow,
Not for a staunch upholder of Christendom,
A stickler for etiquette
A vigilant of moral values
But for a symbol.
A symbol of security and prosperity
Of 'My Country Right or Wrong'
Of 'God is good and Bad is bad'
And 'What was good enough for your father
Ought to be good enough for you'
And 'If you don't eat your tapioca pudding
You will be locked in your bedroom
And given nothing but bread and water
Over and over again until you come to your senses
And are weak and pale and famished and say
Breathlessly, hopelessly and with hate in your heart

"Please Papa I would now like some tapioca pudding very
much indeed" '
A symbol too of proper elegance
Not the flaunting, bejewelled kind
That became so popular
But a truly proper elegance,
An elegance of the spirit,
Of withdrawal from unpleasant subjects
Such as Sex and Poverty and Pit Ponies
And Little Children working in the Mines
And Rude Words and Divorce and Socialism
And numberless other inadmissible horrors.

When Queen Victoria died
They brought her little body from the Isle of Wight
Closed up in a black coffin, finished and done for,
With no longer any feelings and regrets and Memories of Albert
And no more blood pumping through the feeble veins
And no more heart beating away
As it had beaten for so many tiring years.
The coffin was placed upon a gun-carriage
And drawn along sadly and slowly by English sailors.

Noël Coward

Victoria had become a symbol in her own lifetime and the term
'Victorian', as well as denoting a period of history, came to stand for
styles in furniture, architecture, painting, music and morality. Although
Victoria was a constitutional monarch, her longevity and experience
enhanced her personal power – she had, after all, survived sixteen
different Prime Ministers.

The House of Windsor: England in the Twentieth Century

In the twentieth century, Britain had to withstand two world wars which transformed not only its destiny but also that of the whole world. In 1914 Britain, together with France and Russia, had to contain Germany's ambition. Millions of British, French, Germans, Italians and Russians died in the 1914–18 war and slowly the whole world became involved, with troops from Australia, New Zealand, India and America.

The British soldiers did not return to a land fit for heroes and in the 1920s and 1930s Britain was plunged into the Depression with mass unemployment. As the country pulled out of the Depression, Britain was compelled to resist the aggression of Nazi Germany. In 1940 Britain did stand alone against Hitler – our 'finest hour' – but the eventual victory of World War II left the country impoverished.

After the war Britain became a medium-sized power no longer responsible for maintaining the peace of the world. Its economy suffered and it took many years to re-establish prosperity. With memories of the interwar Depression, the Welfare State and the National Health Service were established.

The British Empire was dismantled, beginning with India in 1947, and transformed into the Commonwealth. The countries of Europe decided that they should never again fight against each other and fashioned first a Common Market and then a European Union. Britain had difficulty in adjusting because of its traditional associations with the Commonwealth and America.

No period of one hundred years in the history of the world has seen such dramatic changes. Popular music moved from Gilbert and Sullivan to ragtime, to the Beatles in the sixties, and at the end of the century to Oasis and the Spice Girls. The cinema became a popular pastime, from the silent films to technicolor extravaganzas and ultimately television. In the early 1900s people travelled by horse and carriage, bicycle and train; today we travel by car, motorbike and aeroplane.

King Edward VII, 1901–10

Near Singleton in Sussex you may see
A house of large dimensions on a slope
Diversified by many an ancient tree
And spreading garden lawns of ample scope.
And here it is that, when the Dryads ope
Their first adventurous arms to catch the Spring,
There comes a coronetted envelope,
And Mrs James will entertain the King.

The party will be large and very free,
And people will be given lots of rope,
The Duke of Surrey M.F.H., K.G.
Will bring a *divorcée* in heliotrope.
And Mr Hunt who manufactures soap
Will answer for Victoria, Lady Tring,
And also for Victoria, Lady Scrope;
And Mrs James will entertain the King.

There will be bridge and booze till after three,
And after that a lot of them will grope
Along the passages in *robes de nuit*,
Pyjamas, for another sort of dope.
Sir William Gordon will be set to cope
With some fat dowager; Lord Mainwaring
Will give his wife a third chance to elope;
And Mrs James will entertain the King.
    Envoi
Prince, Father Vaughan will entertain the Pope,
And you will entertain the Jews at Tring,
And I will entertain a pious hope;
And Mrs James will entertain the King.

Hilaire Belloc

The new King had a lively appreciation of the sensual delights of the
world. He smoked twelve large cigars and twenty cigarettes a day.
Dinner for him could run to as many as twelve courses. He enjoyed

grilled oysters and pheasant stuffed with snipe, all washed down with his favourite champagne. He had several mistresses and lady friends who looked after him during those weekend parties for which Edwardian high society was especially noted. Belloc's poem was never published and owes its survival to the memory of Francess Meynell. It dwells on escapades of a weekend spent with Mrs Willie James at West Dean in Sussex; but Mrs Ronald Greville at Polesden Lacey could just as well have provided the pretext.

TWO PRIME MINISTERS

Balfour, 1902-5

The foundations of Philosophic Doubt
Are based on this single premiss:
'Shall we be able to get out
To Wimbledon in time for tennis?'
Rudyard Kipling

Arthur James Balfour became the Conservative Prime Minister in 1902. He was renowned for his indecision, and the title of his first book, *A Defence of Philosophic Doubt*, expresses his whole attitude to life. He was also a keen tennis-player, which led someone to remark: 'His sliced forehand from the base line evoked in him gleams of pale happiness.' Kipling was far harder on him in his prose, describing him as 'arid, aloof, incurious, unthinking, unthanking, gelt'.

Asquith, 1908-16

Mr Asquith says in a manner sweet and calm:
Another little drink wouldn't do us any harm.
George Robey

Herbert Asquith became the Liberal Prime Minister in 1908 and presided over the most talented cabinet of the century – it included Lloyd George and Winston Churchill. Asquith was renowned for his drinking and earned the nickname 'Squiffy'. I remember my history master telling us that he had met Asquith at a dinner in Oxford in the 1920s. Brandy was brought round in glasses on a tray. In the time that it would have taken a student to pick one glass off the tray, Asquith snatched up one and drank it, then a second, which he poured into his coffee, and finally a third, which he kept to put beside his coffee.

EDWARDIAN IDYLLS

Henley Regatta, 1902

Underneath a light straw boater
In his pink Leander tie
Ev'ry ripple in the water caught the Captain in the eye.
O'er the plenitude of houseboats
Plop of punt-poles, creak of rowlocks,
Many a man of some distinction scanned the reach to Temple Island
As a south wind fluttered by,
Till it shifted, westward drifting, strings of pennants house-boat high,
Where unevenly the outline of the brick-warm town of Henley
Dominated by her church tower and the sheds of Brakspear's Brewery
Lay beneath a summer sky.
Plash of sculls! And pink of ices!
And the inn-yards full of ostlers, and the barrels running dry,
And the baskets of geraniums
Swinging over river-gardens
Led us to the flowering heart of England's willow-cooled July.

John Betjeman

After the long, hard slog to imperial greatness under Victoria, social life under Edward VII appears to have been relaxed, happy and indulgent, with great sporting festivals, idyllic country weekends, groaning tables and a general style of plush opulence. But this is only part of the picture. Elsewhere, we must take note of the industrial unrest that was leading to the growth of the Labour Party; of suffragette militancy; of bitter debate as the power of the House of Lords was broken; and of the increasing threat of civil war in Ireland. Yet the sense of a sunny glow over Edwardian England cannot be entirely effaced, and as late as January 1914 Lloyd George could be quoted by the *Daily Chronicle* as saying: 'Never has the sky been more perfectly blue.'

1905

from Haymaking

In the field sloping down,
Park-like, to where the willows showed the brook,
Haymakers rested. The tosser lay forsook
Out in the sun; and the long waggon stood
Without its team: it seemed it never would
Move from the shadow of that single yew.
The team, as still, until their task was due,
Beside the labourers enjoyed the shade
That three squat oaks mid-field together made
Upon a circle of grass and weed uncut,
And on the hollow, once a chalk-pit, but
Now brimmed with nut and elder-flower so clean.
The men leaned on their rakes, about to begin,
But still. And all were silent. All was old,
This morning time, with a great age untold,
Older than Clare and Cobbett, Morland and Crome,
Than, at the field's far edge, the farmer's home
A white house crouched at the foot of a great tree.

Edward Thomas

King George V, 1910–36

THE SUFFRAGETTES

In the Same Boat

Here's to the baby of five or fifteen,
    Here's to the widow of fifty,
Here's to the flaunting extravagant queen,
    And here's to the hussy that's thrifty –
Please to take note, they are in the same boat:
They have not a chance of recording the vote.

Here's to the lunatic, helpless and lost,
    Of wits – well, he simply has none, Sir –
Here's to the woman who lives by her brains
    And is treated as though she were one, Sir –
Please to take note, &c.

Here's to the criminal, lodged in the gaol,
    Voteless for what he has done, Sir –
Here's to the man with a dozen of votes,
    If a woman, he would not have one, Sir –
Please to take note, &c.

Here's to the lot of them, murderer, thief,
    Forger and lunatic too, Sir –
Infants, and those who get parish relief,
    And women, it's perfectly true, Sir –
Please to take note, &c.

H. Crawford

In 1903 Emmeline Pankhurst had formed the Women's Social and
Political Union to promote the cause for Votes for Women. The
campaign was led and conducted by well-educated, well-dressed,
middle-class women – which disconcerted police and politicians alike.
Under their purple, white and green colours, they rallied and marched,
storming Parliament and Downing Street, smashing shop windows,
chaining themselves to railings, mobbing Asquith, attempting to dog-

whip Churchill, and interrupting the meetings of Lloyd George who, on one such occasion, said: 'I see some rats have got in; let them squeal, it doesn't matter.' Many protesters were sent to prison, where they resorted to hunger strikes and were forcibly fed. One brave martyr, Emily Davison, killed herself by jumping in front of George V's horse at the Derby in 1913.

In December 1917 an Electoral Reform Bill was passed in the House of Commons by a large majority and this gave women over thirty the right to vote. In 1928 the age was lowered to twenty-one – the same age as men. It has become a commonplace to suggest that the role which women played in the First World War won them the vote, but Mrs Pankhurst and her two formidable daughters paved the way.

from **The Female of the Species**

When the Himalayan peasant meets the he-bear in his pride,
He shouts to scare the monster, who will often turn aside.
But the she-bear thus accosted rends the peasant tooth and nail.
For the female of the species is more deadly than the male.

Man, a bear in most relations – worm and savage otherwise, –
Man propounds negotiations, Man accepts the compromise.
Very rarely will he squarely push the logic of a fact
To its ultimate conclusion in unmitigated act.

Fear, or foolishness, impels him, ere he lay the wicked low,
To concede some form of trial even to his fiercest foe.
Mirth obscene diverts his anger – Doubt and Pity oft perplex
Him in dealing with an issue – to the scandal of The Sex!

But the Woman that God gave him, every fibre of her frame
Proves her launched for one sole issue, armed and engined for
the same;
And to serve that single issue, lest the generation fail,
The female of the species must be deadlier than the male.

So it comes that Man, the coward, when he gathers to confer
With his fellow-braves in council, dare not leave a place for her
Where, at war with Life and Conscience, he uplifts his erring
hands
To some God of Abstract Justice – which no woman
understands.

And Man knows it! Knows, moreover, that the Woman that God
gave him
Must command but may not govern – shall enthral but not
enslave him.
And *She* knows, because She warns him, and Her instincts
never fail,
That the Female of Her Species is more deadly than the Male.

                                                    Rudyard Kipling

Kipling had little sympathy with the Suffragettes and, when this poem
was printed in the *Morning Post*, he fell out with his daughter over it.
He should have known better, but perhaps the blustering, saloon-bar
style of its argument springs from Kipling's own awkward awareness
of the influence two women in particular – his mother and his wife –
exerted over him.

1912

THE SINKING OF THE 'TITANIC'

The Convergence of the Twain

In a solitude of the sea
Deep from human vanity,
And the Pride of Life that planned her, stilly couches she.

Steel chambers, late the pyres
Of her salamandrine fires,
Cold currents thrid, and turn to rhythmic tidal lyres.

Over the mirrors meant
To glass the opulent
The sea-worm crawls – grotesque, slimed, dumb, indifferent.

Jewels in joy designed
To ravish the sensuous mind
Lie lightless, all their sparkles bleared and black and blind.

Dim moon-eyed fishes near
Gaze at the gilded gear
And query: 'What does this vaingloriousness down here?' . . .

Well: while was fashioning
This creature of cleaving wing,
The Immanent Will that stirs and urges everything

Prepared a sinister mate
For her – so gaily great –
A Shape of Ice, for the time far and dissociate.

And as the smart ship grew
In stature, grace, and hue,
In shadowy silent distance grew the Iceberg too.

Alien they seemed to be:
No mortal eye could see
The intimate welding of their later history,

Or sign that they were bent
By paths coincident
On being anon twin halves of one august event,

Till the Spinner of the Years
Said 'Now!' And each one hears,
And consummation comes, and jars two hemispheres.

Thomas Hardy

The *Titanic* was the grandest ship ever built. On her maiden voyage in 1912 she struck an iceberg and sank with a loss of 1,513 lives. She had been the supreme achievement of Victorian engineering, proof positive of man's triumph over nature, and her tragic fate had a suitably Victorian ring to it: women and children were allowed into the lifeboats first, the band struck up as she sank, and that great hymn 'Nearer, My God, to Thee' was sung. Her loss marked the end of an era.

MCMXIV

Those long uneven lines
Standing as patiently
As if they were stretched outside
The Oval or Villa Park,
The crowns of hats, the sun
On moustached archaic faces
Grinning as if it were all
An August Bank Holiday lark;

And the shut shops, the bleached
Established names on the sunblinds,
The farthings and sovereigns,
And dark-clothed children at play
Called after kings and queens,
The tin advertisements
For cocoa and twist, and the pubs
Wide open all day;

And the countryside not caring:
The place-names all hazed over
With flowering grasses, and fields

Shadowing Domesday lines;
Under wheat's restless silence;
The differently dressed servants
With tiny rooms in huge houses,
The dust behind limousines;

Never such innocence,
Never before or since,
As changed itself to past
Without a word – the men
Leaving the gardens tidy,
The thousands of marriages
Lasting a little while longer:
Never such innocence again.

Philip Larkin

THE FIRST WORLD WAR 1914–1918

The Soldier

If I should die, think only this of me:
That there's some corner of a foreign field
That is for ever England. There shall be
In that rich earth a richer dust concealed;
A dust whom England bore, shaped, made aware,
Gave once her flowers to love, her ways to roam;
A body of England's, breathing English air,
Washed by the rivers, blest by suns of home.

And think, this heart, all evil shed away,
A pulse in the eternal mind, no less
Gives somewhere back the thoughts by England given;
Her sights and sounds; dreams happy as her day;
And laughter, learnt of friends; and gentleness
In hearts at peace, under an English heaven.

Rupert Brooke

In 1914 the major powers in Europe went to war to contain the military ambitions of Germany. The cause was popular, and men flocked to the

colours encouraged by the famous poster showing the pointing
Kitchener and bearing the slogan 'Your Country Needs You'. After the
first few months of swift and traditional fighting, prolonged trench
warfare took over. Generals on both sides sacrificed men and
equipment on a scale unmatched before or since as they attempted to
break through the ranks of the enemy, although this often meant
gaining no more than a few hundred yards. The whole world was
gradually embroiled, with troops pouring in from India, Australia,
New Zealand and eventually America. It was a war that changed
global history. Kingdoms and empires disappeared, the Bolsheviks
assumed power in Russia, and Germany's defeat made the ground
fertile for Nazism. If the leaders of Europe in 1914 could have foreseen
the state of the continent twenty years later, every one of them would
have done all that was possible to avoid war. The catastrophe, however,
produced some of the finest poetry of the twentieth century, and the
poems can be left to speak for themselves.

Dulce Et Decorum Est

Bent double, like old beggars under sacks,
Knock-kneed, coughing like hags, we cursed through sludge,
Till on the haunting flares we turned our backs,
And towards our distant rest began to trudge.
Men marched asleep. Many had lost their boots,
But limped on, blood-shod. All went lame, all blind;
Drunk with fatigue; deaf even to the hoots
Of gas-shells dropping softly behind.

Gas! Gas! Quick, boys! – An ecstasy of fumbling,
Fitting the clumsy helmets just in time,
But someone still was yelling out and stumbling
And floundering like a man in fire or lime. –
Dim through the misty panes and thick green light,
As under a green sea, I saw him drowning.

In all my dreams, before my helpless sight,
He plunges at me, guttering, choking, drowning.

If in some smothering dreams, you too could pace
Behind the wagon that we flung him in,
And watch the white eyes writhing in his face,

His hanging face, like a devil's sick of sin;
If you could hear, at every jolt, the blood
Come gargling from the froth-corrupted lungs,
Obscene as cancer, bitter as the cud
Of vile, incurable sores on innocent tongues, –
My friend, you would not tell with such high zest
To children ardent for some desperate glory,
The old Lie: Dulce et decorum est
Pro patria mori.

Wilfred Owen

The General

'Good-morning, good-morning!' the General said
When we met him last week on our way to the line.
Now the soldiers he smiled at are most of 'em dead,
And we're cursing his staff for incompetent swine.
'He's a cheery old card,' grunted Harry to Jack
As they slogged up to Arras with rifle and pack.

But he did for them both by his plan of attack.

Siegfried Sassoon

For the Fallen
(1914)

With proud thanksgiving, a mother for her children,
England mourns for her dead across the sea.
Flesh of her flesh they were, spirit of her spirit,
Fallen in the cause of the free.

Solemn the drums thrill: Death august and royal
Sings sorrow up into immortal spheres.
There is music in the midst of desolation
And a glory that shines upon our tears.

They went with songs to the battle, they were young,
Straight of limb, true of eye, steady and aglow.

They were staunch to the end against odds uncounted,
They fell with their faces to the foe.

They shall grow not old, as we that are left grow old:
Age shall not weary them, nor the years condemn.
At the going down of the sun and in the morning
We will remember them.

They mingle not with their laughing comrades again;
They sit no more at familiar tables of home;
They have no lot in our labour of the day-time;
They sleep beyond England's foam.

Laurence Binyon

Elegy in a Country Churchyard

The men that worked for England
They have their graves at home:
And bees and birds of England
About the cross can roam.

But they that fought for England,
Following a falling star,
Alas, alas for England
They have their graves afar.

And they that rule in England,
In stately conclave met,
Alas, alas for England
They have no graves as yet.

G. K. Chesterton

SOME MINISTERS OF THE TWENTIETH CENTURY

David Lloyd George, PM 1916–22

Count not his broken pledges as a crime
He MEANT them, HOW he meant them – at the time.

Kensal Green

Andrew Bonar Law, PM 1922–3

Of all the politicians I ever saw
The least significant was Bonar Law.
Unless it was MacDonald, by the way:
Or Baldwin – it's impossible to say.

Hilaire Belloc

Stanley Baldwin, PM 1923–4, 1924–9, 1935–7

His fame endures; we shall not quite forget
The name of Baldwin till we're out of debt.

Kensal Green

Winston Churchill, PM 1940–5, 1951–5

A sad day this for Alexander
And many another dead commander.
Jealousy's rife in heroes' hall –
Winston Churchill has bluffed them all.

Kensal Green

the 1920s

A LAND FIT FOR HEROES

**Refutation of the Only Too Prevalent Slander that
Parliamentary Leaders are Indifferent to the Strict Fulfilment
of their Promises and the Preservation of their Reputation
for Veracity**

They said (when they had dined at Ciro's)
The land would soon be fit for heroes;
And now they've managed to ensure it,
For only heroes could endure it.

G. K. Chesterton

1926

THE GENERAL STRIKE

May 4th, 1926

May 4th, 1926 – morning,
East End classroom crowded
With youth and feeling unconfined,
Crimson ties proclaiming oneness
With workers – red flags fluttering
In the corridors of the mind.
To bull-like masters red rags,
Well-worn beyond those cockcrow years,
Beyond betrayals and disasters;
Remembrance that the battering shower
Of time, its storms can never nip.
Among her festivals and bitter tears
Comes home this memory
Like a well-laden, triumphant ship.

Bill Foot

On 1 May 1926, after a prolonged dispute over a miners' wage claim, to which colliery owners had responded by offering a reduction in wages, there was a lock-out. The General Council of the Trade Unions declared a national strike from 3 May, and this was widely supported. Stanley Baldwin, Prime Minister of the day, urged Winston Churchill to bring out a daily paper under the name of the *British Gazette*, in which he called for 'unconditional surrender'. Many people volunteered to keep basic services going. Throughout all this, George V played a moderating role and, when the strike was called off unconditionally, Baldwin resisted any vindictive inclination to turn the affair into a class-war victory.

THE MINERS ON STRIKE

What will you do with your shovel, Dai,
And your pick and your sledge and your spike,
And what will you do with your leisure, man,
Now that you're out on strike?

What will you do for your butter, Dai,
And your bread and your cheese and your fags,
And how will you pay for a dress for the wife,
And shall your children go in rags?

You have been, in your time, a hero, Dai,
And they wrote of your pluck in the press,
And now you have fallen on evil days,
And who will be there to bless?

And how will you stand with your honesty, Dai,
When the land is full of lies,
And how will you curb your anger, man,
When your natural patience dies?

O what will you dream on the mountains, Dai,
When you walk in the summer day,
And gaze on the derelict valleys below,
And the mountains farther away?

> And how will the heart within you, Dai,
> Respond to the distant sea,
> And the dream that is born in the blaze of the sun,
> And the vision of victory?

Idris Davies

The post-war boom soon petered out and unemployment rose to one million, 12 per cent of the British work force. In 1929, particularly as a result of the Wall Street Crash and the collapse of financial institutions in America, unemployment rose sharply to three million. Everyone was at a loss. The Coalition Government under the Labour leader, Ramsay MacDonald, wanted to cut benefits; the influential economist John Maynard Keynes advocated public works; others urged protection. Neville Chamberlain, as Chancellor of the Exchequer, nursed the economy back to health and by 1937 unemployment had been cut by half.

1936

The Death of King George V

> 'New King arrives in his capital by air . . .'
> *Daily Newspaper*

Spirits of well-shot woodcock, partridge, snipe
  Flutter and bear him up the Norfolk sky:
In that red house in a red mahogany book-case
  The stamp collection waits with mounts long dry.

The big blue eyes are shut which saw wrong clothing
  And favourite fields and coverts from a horse;
Old men in country houses hear clocks ticking
  Over thick carpets with a deadened force;

Old men who never cheated, never doubted,
  Communicated monthly, sit and stare
At the new suburb stretched beyond the run-way
  Where a young man lands hatless from the air.

John Betjeman

At Sandringham on the evening of 20 January 1936 the King's doctor, Lord Dawson of Penn, wrote this last bulletin on a menu card: 'The King's life is moving peacefully to its close.' Three hours later George V was dead. It was only in 1986 that the notes of Dawson were published to reveal that he had administered euthanasia. 'At about 11 o'clock', Dawson wrote, 'it was evident that the last stage might endure for many hours unknown to the patient, but little comporting with that dignity and serenity which he so richly merited and which demanded a brief final scene . . . I therefore decided myself to determine the end and injected myself morphia gr. $\frac{3}{4}$ and shortly afterwards cocaine gr. 1 into the distended jugular vein.' This meant that the King's death would first be announced 'in the morning papers rather than the less appropriate field of the evening journals'. Dawson had been the doctor of Edward VII and also of Lloyd George, who had insisted on his being made a peer in 1920. He had saved the King's life in 1928, but his treatment during the convalescence led to a good deal of professional jealousy and this piece of doggerel:

> Lord Dawson of Penn
> Has killed lots of men.
> So that's why we sing
> God save the King.

King Edward VIII, 1936

The hand that blew the sacred fire has failed,
Laid down the burden in the hour of need,
So brave begun but flinching in the deed.
Nor Mary's power nor Baldwin's word availed,
To curb the beating heart by love assailed.
Vainly did Delhi, Canberra, Capetown plead
The Empire's ruler flouts the Empire's creed
By princes, prelates, people sore bewailed
The triple pillars of the Empire shake
A shock of horror passes o'er the land.
The greatest throne in all the world forsake
To take a favour from a woman's hand?
The hallowed pleasures of a kingly life
Abandoned for a transatlantic wife.

Douglas Reed

Edward VIII ruled for 11 months – the shortest reign in English history, if one overlooks that of Lady Jane Grey. Edward had fallen in love with Wallis Simpson, an American, who had been married twice before and was about to divorce her second husband. As head of the Church of England, Edward could not marry Mrs Simpson and remain on the throne. The country was divided. Beaverbrook and Churchill supported the King, while Baldwin and Archbishop Lang forced him to the realization that he had to make a choice. He chose to abdicate.

My Lord Archbishop, what a scold you are,
And when a man is down, how bold you are,
Of Christian charity how scant you are
You auld Lang Swine, how full of cant you are!

Anonymous

King George VI, 1936–52

THE BLACKSHIRTS

October 1936

We stood at Gardiner's Corner,
We stood and watched the crowds,
We stood at Gardiner's Corner,
Firm, solid, voices loud.

Came the marching of the blackshirts,
Came the pounding of their feet,
Came the sound of ruffians marching
Where the five roads meet.

We thought of many refugees
Fleeing from the Fascist hordes,
The maimed, the sick,
The young, the old,
Those who had fought the Fascist lords.

So we stopped them there at Gardiner's,
We fought and won our way.

> We fought the baton charges,
> No Fascist passed that day!
>
> *Milly Harris*

About 3,000 black-shirted Fascists, under the leadership of Oswald Mosley, were to have marched through the East End of London on 4 October 1936 – a calculated affront to its large Jewish population. The residents, however, blocked the roads at Gardiner's Corner and Cable Street, and Mosley was ignominiously forced to lead his men elsewhere. The following poem, written in the early years of the Second World War, shows the strength of Jewish identification with that part of London.

Whitechapel in Britain

> Pumbedita, Cordova, Cracow, Amsterdam,
> Vilna, Lublin, Berditchev and Volozhin,
> Your names will always be sacred,
> Places where Jews have been.
>
> And sacred is Whitechapel,
> It is numbered with our Jewish towns.
> Holy, holy, holy
> Are your bombed stones.
>
> If we ever have to leave Whitechapel,
> As other Jewish towns were left,
> Its soul will remain a part of us,
> Woven into us, woof and weft.
>
> *Avram Stencl*

Throughout its history, England has welcomed many waves of political refugees: Huguenots came from France in the seventeenth century; Armenians in the nineteenth century; and Jews from Germany and Russia in the twentieth century. Many settled in the East End of London as it was the only place they could afford to live. In recent years, other immigrant groups from the West Indies, India and Pakistan have moved into Whitechapel and other parts of East London. The Jewish communities have moved further out.

1938

THE MUNICH AGREEMENT

from **Autumn Journal**

And the next day begins
  Again with alarm and anxious
Listening to bulletins
  From distant, measured voices
Arguing for peace
  While the zero hour approaches,
While the eagles gather and the petrol and oil and grease
  Have all been applied and the vultures back the eagles.
But once again
  The crisis is put off and things look better
And we feel negotiation is not vain –
  Save my skin and damn my conscience.
And negotiation wins,
  If you can call it winning,
And here we are – just as before – safe in our skins;
  Glory to God for Munich.
And stocks go up and wrecks
  Are salved and politicians' reputations
Go up like Jack-on-the Beanstalk; only the Czechs
  Go down and without fighting.

Louis MacNeice

In 1938 the Conservative Prime Minister, Neville Chamberlain, came to terms with Adolf Hitler over the German leader's provocative seizure of a part of Czechoslovakia. Chamberlain flew back from Munich with the confident boast that he had secured 'peace in our time'. He was the hero of the hour, and all the press supported him, with the exception of the left-wing Sunday newspaper *Reynolds' News*. Duff Cooper was the only Cabinet minister to resign and only thirty Conservative MPs abstained from voting for the agreement. Six months before Munich, Hilaire Belloc had told Duff Cooper that Chamberlain had written this poem:

> Dear Czecho-Slovakia,
> I don't think they'll attack yer,
> But I'm not going to back yer.

The Second World War 1939–1945

A LOW DISHONEST DECADE

from **September 1, 1939**

I sit in one of the dives
On Fifty-Second Street
Uncertain and afraid
As the clever hopes expire
Of a low dishonest decade:
Waves of anger and fear
Circulate over the bright
And darkened lands of the earth,
Obsessing our private lives;
The unmentionable odour of death
Offends the September night.

Accurate scholarship can
Unearth the whole offence
From Luther until now
That has driven a culture mad,
Find what occurred at Linz,
What huge imago made
A psychopathic god:
I and the public know
What all schoolchildren learn,
Those to whom evil is done
Do evil in return.

Exiled Thucydides knew
All that a speech can say
About Democracy,
And what dictators do,
The elderly rubbish they talk,
To an apathetic grave;
Analysed all in his book,
The enlightenment driven away,

The habit-forming pain,
Mismanagement and grief:
We must suffer them all again.

All I have is a voice
To undo the folded lie,
The romantic lie in the brain
Of the sensual man-in-the-street
And the lie of Authority
Whose buildings grope the sky:
There is no such thing as the State
And no one exists alone;
Hunger allows no choice
To the citizen or the police;
We must love one another or die.

Defenceless under the night
Our world in stupor lies;
Yet, dotted everywhere,
Ironic points of light
Flash out wherever the Just
Exchange their messages:
May I, composed like them
Of Eros and of dust,
Beleaguered by the same
Negation and despair,
Show an affirming flame.

W. H. Auden

By 1939, attempts to check Hitler's plans of expansion had led nowhere. In August of that year Russia and Germany signed a neutrality pact, both hoping to seize for themselves large parts of Poland; and on 1 September Germany invaded Poland. Reluctantly yielding to pressure from a hostile House of Commons – from the Labour Party under its acting leader Arthur Greenwood, and from his own Cabinet – Chamberlain issued an ultimatum demanding German withdrawal by midnight on 2 September. On the following day, when it was clear that this had been ignored, he declared that Britain was at war. It was a justified war, as the Nazi regime in Germany was one of the worst and most cruel tyrannies the world had ever seen.

After the fall of France in June 1940, Britain stood alone in opposing the German offensive. Churchill had by then succeeded Chamberlain as Prime Minister and, in prose as memorable as any poetry, choosing 18 June, the anniversary of the battle of Waterloo, as a suitable moment, he addressed the nation in a speech which included the sentence: 'Let us therefore brace ourselves to our duties, and so bear ourselves that, if the British Empire and its Commonwealth last for a thousand years, men will still say, "This was their finest hour".'

In 1941 Hitler made the decisive mistake of invading Russia, and when the Japanese destroyed an American fleet in Pearl Harbor it became a real world war. From it emerged two pre-eminent global powers, Russia and America. Germany itself was divided in two, and the states of Eastern Europe became Russian satellites. Britain had won a famous victory, but post-war adjustment to a less dominant position in the world was to prove painful.

1940

In Westminster Abbey

Let me take this other glove off
    As the *vox humana* swells,
And the beauteous fields of Eden
    Bask beneath the Abbey bells.
Here, where England's statesmen lie,
Listen to a lady's cry.

Gracious Lord, oh bomb the Germans.
    Spare their women for Thy Sake.
And if that is not too easy
    We will pardon Thy Mistake.
But, gracious Lord, whate'er shall be,
Don't let anyone bomb me.

Keep our Empire undismembered
    Guide our Forces by Thy Hand,
Gallant blacks from far Jamaica,
    Honduras and Togoland;
Protect them Lord in all their fights,
And, even more, protect the whites.

Think of what our Nation stands for,
    Books from Boots' and country lanes,

Free speech, free passes, class distinction,
    Democracy and proper drains.
Lord, put beneath Thy special care
One-eighty-nine Cadogan Square.

Although dear Lord I am a sinner,
    I have done no major crime;
Now I'll come to Evening Service
    Whensoever I have the time.
So, Lord, reserve for me a crown;
And do not let my shares go down.

I will labour for Thy Kingdom,
    Help our lads to win the war,
Send white feathers to the cowards
    Join the Women's Army Corps,
Then wash the Steps around Thy Throne
In the Eternal Safety Zone.

Now I feel a little better,
    What a treat to hear Thy Word,
Where the bones of leading statesmen,
    Have so often been interr'd.
And now, dear Lord, I cannot wait
Because I have a luncheon date.

                              John Betjeman

THE RETREAT FROM DUNKIRK

That night we blew our guns. We placed a shell
Fuze downwards in each muzzle. Then we put
Another in the breech, secured a wire
Fast to the firing lever, crouched, and pulled.
It sounded like a cry of agony,
The crash and clang of splitting, tempered steel.
Thus did our guns, our treasured colours, pass;
And we were left bewildered, weaponless,
And rose and marched, our faces to the sea.

We formed in line beside the water's edge.
The little waves made oddly home-like sounds,
Breaking in half-seen surf upon the strand.
The night was full of noise; the whistling thud
The shells made in the sand, and pattering stones;
The cries cut short, the shouts of units' names;
The crack of distant shots, and bren gun fire;
The sudden clattering crash of masonry.
Steadily, all the time, the marching tramp
Of feet passed by along the shell-torn road,
Under the growling thunder of the guns.

The major said 'The boats cannot get in,
There is no depth of water. Follow me.'
And so we followed, wading in our ranks
Into the blackness of the sea. And there,
Lit by the burning oil across the swell,
We stood and waited for the unseen boats.

Oars in the darkness, rowlocks, shadowy shapes
Of boats that searched. We heard a seaman's hail.
Then we swam out, and struggled with our gear,
Clutching the looming gunwales. Strong hands pulled,
And we were in and heaving with the rest,
Until at last they turned. The dark oars dipped,
The laden craft crept slowly out to sea,
To where in silence lay the English ships.

B. G. Bonallack

On 10 May 1940 the allied armies advanced into German-occupied
Holland, but within five days the Dutch had surrendered and German
troops swept through Northern France as far as the outskirts of Paris.
The British army of ten divisions had been cut off by this advance and
fell back to the coast. The Germans halted their attack on the British on
23 May, allowing an opportunity for evacuation from the port of
Dunkirk. On 27 May the British fleet began to pick men up from the
beaches, helped by an enormous flotilla of private boats – pleasure
steamers, ferries, fishing vessels and so on. In all, 860 boats were able to
rescue 338,226 men, 139,000 of them French. Most equipment had been
sunk and 474 planes were lost. In immediate military terms, it was a
great disaster, but it saved Britain from an even greater one. In his
report to the House of Commons on 4 June, Churchill declared: 'We

shall defend our Island whatever the cost may be. We shall fight on the beaches, we shall fight on the landing grounds, we shall fight in the fields and in the streets, we shall fight in the hills; we shall never surrender, and even if, which I do not for a moment believe, this Island or a large part of it were subjugated and starving, then our Empire beyond the seas, armed and guarded by the British fleet, would carry on the struggle, until, in God's good time, the New World, with all its power and might, steps forth to the rescue and liberation of the Old.'

THE BATTLE OF BRITAIN

For Johnny

Do not despair
For Johnny-head-in-air;
He sleeps as sound
As Johnny underground.

Fetch out no shroud
For Johnny-in-the-cloud;
And keep your tears
For him in after years.

Better by far
For Johnny-the-bright-star,
To keep your head,
And see his children fed.

John Pudney

After Dunkirk, Hitler prepared to invade Britain. He started by launching Goering's Luftwaffe on a campaign of bombing raids. British pilots, mostly flying Spitfires, took off from the small airfields of southern and eastern England and succeeded in destroying many of the German bombers. In August the Luftwaffe came close to wiping out the airfields of Kent, but on 7 September it switched its attack to London. Air Marshall Dowding's fighter-pilots brought down 1,733 German planes, while the RAF lost 915. The bravery of these pilots saved Britain and on 17 September Hitler postponed his invasion. Churchill reported to the House of Commons: 'Never in the field of human conflict was so much owed by so many to so few.' The architect of the victory, Dowding, was removed from his command in November, Churchill having found him too cautious, but history has accorded him due honours.

THE BLITZ

London, 1940

After fourteen hours clearing they came to him
Under the twisted girders and the rubble.
They would not let me see his face.
Now I sit shiftlessly on the tube platforms
Or huddle, a little tipsy, in brick-built shelters.
I can see with an indifferent eye
The red glare over by the docks and hear
Impassively the bomb-thuds in the distance.

For me, a man with not many interests
And no pretensions to fame, that was my world,
My son of fifteen, my only concrete achievement,
Whom they could not protect. Stepping aside
From the Great Crusade, I will play the idiot's part.
You, if you like, may wave your fists and crash
On the wrong doorsteps brash retaliation.

Frank Thompson

On 7 September German air force commander Hermann Goering
assumed personal command of the air offensive and directed his planes

against London, which was bombed for fifty-seven consecutive nights.
Each night 220 planes dropped incendiary as well as explosive bombs,
causing widespread damage. The House of Commons was destroyed,
Buckingham Palace was hit, and 30,000 civilians were killed.
Londoners slept on the platforms of Underground stations, sandbags
were piled around windows, and I remember spending the night under
our stairs, which was considered the safest place in the house, and on
some occasions being taken out to an air-raid shelter. Other cities
besides London were also attacked: Coventry lost 1,236 civilians,
Birmingham 2,162, Bristol 1,159, Sheffield 624, and Manchester 1,005.
On 29 December the great onslaught on the City of London destroyed
eight Wren churches and almost St Paul's Cathedral itself. George VI
remained in London throughout the Blitz, as did Churchill, and their
example helped stiffen the morale of the people.

Naming Of Parts

Today we have naming of parts. Yesterday,
We had daily cleaning. And tomorrow morning,
We shall have what to do after firing. But today,
Today we have naming of parts. Japonica
Glistens like coral in all of the neighbouring gardens,
    And today we have naming of parts.

This is the lower sling swivel. And this
Is the upper sling swivel, whose use you will see,
When you are given your slings. And this is the piling swivel,
Which in your case you have not got. The branches
Hold in the gardens their silent, eloquent gestures,
    Which in our case we have not got.

This is the safety-catch, which is always released
With an easy flick of the thumb. And please do not let me
See anyone using his finger. You can do it quite easy
If you have any strength in your thumb. The blossoms
Are fragile and motionless, never letting anyone see
    Any of them using their finger.

And this you can see is the bolt. The purpose of this
Is to open the breech, as you see. We can slide it
Rapidly backwards and forwards: we call this

Easing the spring. And rapidly backwards and forwards
The early bees are assaulting and fumbling the flowers:
   They call it easing the Spring.

They call it easing the Spring: it is perfectly easy
If you have any strength in your thumb: like the bolt,
And the breech, and the cocking-piece, and the point of balance,
Which in our case we have not got; and the almond-blossom
Silent in all of the gardens and the bees going backwards and
    forwards,
   For today we have naming of parts.

Henry Reed

1940–2

THE WAR IN THE WESTERN DESERT

Vergissmeinnicht

Three weeks gone and the combatants gone
returning over the nightmare ground
we found the place again, and found
the soldier sprawling in the sun.

The frowning barrel of his gun
overshadowing. As we came on
that day, he hit my tank with one
like the entry of a demon.

Look. Here in the gunpit spoil
the dishonoured picture of his girl
who has put: *Steffi. Vergissmeinnicht*
in a copybook gothic script.

We see him almost with content,
abased, and seeming to have paid
and mocked at by his own equipment
that's hard and good when he's decayed.

But she would weep to see today
how on his skin the swart flies move;

the dust upon the paper eye
and the burst stomach like a cave.

For here the lover and killer are mingled
who had one body and one heart.
And death who had the soldier singled
has done the lover mortal hurt.

Keith Douglas

Britain had a large army in Egypt and in 1940 won spectacular victories
when it pushed Germany's Italian allies out of most of modern-day
Libya. Germany came to Italy's help and their armies were brilliantly
led by Field Marshall Rommel, the 'Desert Fox'. There were wide-
ranging battles involving armoured tanks and infantry – just the sort of
battles that soldiers of the time had been trained to fight. Rommel
pushed the British troops back and in June 1942 Tobruk, on the borders
of Egypt, fell to his advance. Field Marshall Montgomery, who was
appointed to command the 8th Army, proved a match for Rommel. He
was a great field commander and a charismatic leader who soon won
the devotion of his troops. Rommel was forced to evacuate North
Africa and his retreat took him through Sicily and Italy.

The German title of Keith Douglas's poem means 'forget-me-not'.

1945

VJ DAY

The Morning After

The fire left to itself might smoulder weeks.
Phone cables melt. Paint peels from off back gates.
Kitchen windows crack; the whole street reeks
of horsehair blazing. Still it celebrates.

Though people weep, their tears dry from the heat.
Faces flush with flame, beer, sheer relief
and such a sense of celebration in our street
for me it still means joy though banked with grief.

And that, now clouded, sense of public joy
with war-worn adults wild in their loud fling

has never come again since as a boy
I saw Leeds people dance and heard them sing.

There's still that dark, scorched circle on the road.
The morning after kids like me helped spray
hissing upholstery spring-wire that still glowed
and cobbles boiling with black gas-tar for VJ.

Tony Harrison

America dropped two atom bombs on Japan in 1945 – one at Hiroshima on 8 August, and the other at Nagasaki on 29 August. Four days later Japan surrendered and that ended the war. There were parties and street celebrations all over Britain, and I can remember attending a huge bonfire party in Newport which local residents had quickly organized.

1945–51

THE PREMIERSHIP OF CLEMENT ATTLEE

Few thought he was even a starter;
There were many who thought themselves smarter;
But he ended PM,
CH and OM,
An Earl and a Knight of the Garter.

Clement Attlee

from Lest Cowards Flinch

1945

'Though cowards flinch,' the Labour Party trolled
  'The people's scarlet standard we will raise!'
The Commons blushed beneath that sanguine fold,
  Flag of the revolutionary phase;
The Tories knew for whom the death-bell tolled,
  It tolled for them in Labour's *Marseillaise*,
And in the beat of that triumphant march
Heard tumbrils rumbling up to Marble Arch.

Grim was it in that dawn to be alive,
    Except to those who like their mornings bloody,
The ship of State headlong was seen to dive
    Engulfed in depths unutterly muddy,
As *Jacobins*, like swarms that leave the hive,
    Belched forth from foundry, factory and study,
A cut-throat crew of howling demagogues,
Leading hereditary underdogs.

1947

Two years of Parliamentary civility
    Abate the class, if not the Party, feud;
No Labour Member lacks respectability,
    Although his social background may be rude,
While several have a title to gentility
    Such as the Tory ranks might not exclude,
And manual labourers, if fairly prominent,
On the Front Bench at least are not predominant.

Both birth and intellect are there displayed;
    The Premier is impeccably Oxonian,
A younger son conducts the Board of Trade,
    The Chancellor's a perfect Old Etonian,
The Foreign Secretary, though self-made,
    Is quite magnificently Palmerstonian;
If such as these are Labour mediocrities,
Where is the Tory Cicero, or Socrates?

                                        Sagittarius

In July 1945 the British electorate decisively snubbed its wartime leader, Churchill, by returning 393 Socialist MPs and only 213 Conservatives. Consoled by his wife, Clementine, that the defeat could be interpreted as a blessing in disguise, Churchill retorted that the disguise was perfect. Under Attlee, the Socialist Government nationalized the Bank of England and several major industries, and it set up the National Health Service. Its achievements marked the high tide of Socialism in Britain. On the first day of the new Parliament, the Socialist MPs rose and sang 'The Red Flag'. Less than half of their number would have called themselves working-class, and forty-six had been educated at either Oxford or Cambridge.

Sagittarius was the *nom de plume* of the prolific topical poet, Olga Katzin Miller.

1947

THE END OF THE EMPIRE

Partition

Unbiased at least he was when he arrived on his mission.
Having never set eyes on this land he was called to partition
Between two peoples fanatically at odds,
With their different diets and incompatible gods.
'Time,' they had briefed him in London, 'is short. It's too late
For mutual reconciliation or rational debate;
The only solution now lies in separation.
The Viceroy thinks, as you see from his letter,
That the less you are seen in his company the better.
So we've arranged to provide you with other accommodation.
We can give you four judges, two Moslem and two Hindu,
To consult with but the final decision must rest with you.'

Shut up in a lonely mansion, with police night and day
Patrolling the gardens to keep assassins away,
He got down to work, to the task of settling the fate
Of millions. The maps at his disposal were out of date
And the Census Returns almost certainly incorrect.
But there was no time to check them, no time to inspect
Contested areas. The weather was frightfully hot.
And a bout of dysentery kept him constantly on the trot.
But in seven weeks it was done, the frontiers decided,
A continent for better or worse divided.

The next day he sailed for England, where he quickly forged
The case, as a good lawyer must. Return he would not.
Afraid, as he told his Club, that he might get shot.

                                        W. H. Auden

Britain's rule in India came to an end at midnight on 14 August 1947.
As the Indian leader Nehru put it: 'At the stroke of midnight when the
world sleeps India will wake to life and freedom.' Mahatma Gandhi, a
driving force behind the move towards independence, did not join in

the celebrations as he was strongly opposed to the partition of India and Pakistan. The birth of these new states was not accomplished without pain, for hundreds of thousands of Muslims and Hindus were killed in communal violence and there were millions of refugees. Britain left behind a language which was to serve for communication in all parts of that vast sub-continent, an established bureaucracy, now lovingly embellished, and a democratic system of government. The legacy has stood up well. Many former colonial servants and old soldiers 'stayed on', but things were never to be the same for them.

Epilogue To An Empire 1600–1900

An Ode For Trafalgar Day

As I was crossing Trafalgar Square
whose but the Admiral's shadow hand
should tap my shoulder. At my ear:
'You Sir, stay-at-home citizen
poet, here's more use for your pen
than picking scabs. Tell them in England
this: when first I stuck my head in the air,

'winched from a cockpit's tar and blood
to my crow's nest over London, I
looked down on a singular crowd
moving with the confident swell
of the sea. As it rose and fell every pulse in the estuary
carried them quayward, carried them seaward.

'Box-wallah, missionary, clerk,
lancer, planter, I saw them all
linked like the waves on the waves embark.
Their eyes looked out – as yours look in –
to harbour names on the cabin-trunks
carrying topees to Bengal,
maxims or gospels to lighten a dark

'continent. Blatant as the flag
they went out under were the bright
abstractions nailed to every mast.
Sharpshooters since have riddled most

and buried an empire in their rags –
scrivener, do you dare to write
a little 'e' in the epilogue

'to an empire that spread its wings
wider than Rome? They are folded,
you say, with the maps and flags; awnings
and verandahs overrun
by impis of the ant; sun-
downers sunk, and the planters' blood
turned tea or siphoned into rubber saplings.

'My one eye reports that their roads
remain, their laws, their language
seeding all winds. They were no gods
from harnessed clouds, as the islanders
thought them, nor were they monsters
but men, as you stooped over your page
and you and you and these wind-driven crowds

'are and are not. For you have lost
their rhythm, the pulse of the sea
in their salt blood. Your heart has missed
the beat of centuries, its channels
silted to their source. The muscles
of the will stricken by distrophy
dishonour those that bareback rode the crest

'of untamed seas. Acknowledge
their energy. If you condemn
their violence in a violent age
speak of their courage. Mock their pride
when, having built as well, in as wide
a compass, you have none. Tell them
in England this.'

And a pigeon sealed the page.

Jon Stallworthy

1950

THE GENERAL ELECTION

Parties drilled for the election,
All accoutred to perfection,
March for national inspection,
    Parties on parade!
Labour's serried ranks resplendent,
Tories with their aims transcendant,
Liberals, proudly independent,
    CP shock brigade.

Attlee in the saddle seated,
With his five year term completed,
Heads his cohorts undefeated,
    Near four hundred strong!
All the Party regimented,
Toryism circumvented,
All constituents contented
    Cheering loud and long.

Winston on his war-horse bounding,
With the Tory trumpets sounding,
After last election's pounding,
    His two hundred leads;
Eden, next in the succession,
Fighting forces of oppression,
With Young Tories, in procession,
    Also cheered, proceeds.

Bearers of the Liberal Charter!
Clement Davies is the starter,
Pressed by Lady Bonham Carter
    And McFadyean's men.
In the Liberal tradition
All condemn to demolition
Government and Opposition
    (Sitting Members, ten).

Voters, it's no time to dally!
None must shirk or shilly-shally!
To your chosen Party rally
     As for power they strive.
If too long you hesitate, or
If the ballot you are late for,
Voters, you will have to wait for
     1955.

Sagittarius

The Labour Government had weathered many storms: the devaluation
of sterling, a fuel crisis in the severe winter of 1947, and a flourishing
black market brought about by rationing. Yet since 1945 they had lost
not a single by-election. At the general election of 1950, however, they
took office again with a majority of only six over all other parties. Attlee
soldiered on for a further eighteen months, until in 1951 he was
defeated by Churchill, who was returned with a majority of seventeen.
The people were tired of austerity and, under R. A. Butler's guidance,
the Tory party presented a more attractive programme attuned to the
requirements of post-war Britain.

1951

THE FESTIVAL OF BRITAIN

from **Don't Make Fun of the Fair**

Don't make fun of the festival,
Don't make fun of the fair,
We down-trodden British must learn to be skittish
And give an impression of devil-may-care
To the wide wide world,
We'll sing 'God for Harry',
And if it turns out all right
Knight Gerald Barry,
Clear the national decks, my lads,
Everyone of us counts,
Grab the traveller's cheques, my lads,
And pray that none of them bounce.

Boys and Girls come out to play,
Every day in every way
Help the tourist to defray
All that's underwritten.
Sell your rations and overcharge,
And don't let anyone sabotage
Our own dear Festival of Britain.

Don't make fun of the festival,
Don't make fun of the fair,
We must pull together in spite of the weather
That dampens our spirits and straightens our hair.
Let the people sing
Even though they shiver
Roses red and noses mauve
Over the river.

Though the area's fairly small,
Climb Discovery's Dome,
Take a snooze in the concert hall,
At least it's warmer than home.
March about in funny hats,
Show the foreign diplomats
That our proletariat's
Milder than a kitten.

We believe in the right to strike,
But now we've bloody well got to like
Our own dear festival of Britain.

Noël Coward

The Labour Party, largely at the instigation of Herbert Morrison,
decided to try to cheer everyone up by holding a national festival on
the South Bank of the Thames, where a brewery had to be pulled down
and a tall chimney, once a shot tower, demolished to make room for the
site. A celebratory exhibition was held in the Dome of Discovery,
erected at the centre alongside a great cigar-shaped construction
pointing into the sky and called the Skylon. The one permanent thing
to come out of the Festival was the Festival Hall, which looks as if it
may last a bit longer than the Crystal Palace. The stone lion which had
adorned the brewery now stands at the southern end of Westminster
Bridge.

Queen Elizabeth II, 1952–

1953

THE CORONATION OF ELIZABETH II

In a golden coach
There's a heart of gold
   That belongs to you and me.
And one day in June
When the flowers are in bloom
   That day will make history.
                    Donald Jamieson

The song from which this verse is taken was sung by Dickie Valentine and 200,000 copies of the record were sold. Another popular song of the time included the words:

Everybody's mad about ya
Where would Britain be without ya?
Sailing in the yacht Britannia
Nowhere in the world would ban ya.
Queenie Baby, I'm not foolin',
Only you could do the ruling,
In your own sweet royal way.

the 1950s

Ancient and Modern

Back in 1950
when Mums did Palais Glides
and girls still got an earful
from Dad's short back and sides

and creamy capuccino
overlaid the tongue

with sweet and sexy flavours
and pop was Jimmy Young

and sweets came off the ration
and jazz sprang up in dives
and Comets screamed on newsreels
and Woodbines came in fives

and Tories ruled forever
and Empire meant Free Trade
and intellectuals took their stand
in corduroy and suede

and BBC announcers
said Churchill won applors
and Rank rebuffed Jane Russell
with young Diana Dors

and George gave way to Lizbet
and LPs offered gems
as the Festival of Britain
played sweetly by the Thames

and Compton creamed the bowlers
and Longhurst opened up
and Sunset fell at Beecher's
and Matthews won the Cup

and lady Docker's Daimler
glistened in the mews
and Beaverbrook lost Suez
and Dylan found his muse

and Humph blew infant solos
and Eden made it clear
that only a rich man ever earned
a thousand pounds a year

they brought *you* into being
yes, eyes and nose and chin
all set to smile and play, as if
the past had never been

and parents were for leaving
and history was bunk
and every kind of loving
was money in the bank!

William Scammell

1960s

I Love Me Mudder (Mother) . . .

I love me mudder and me mudder love me
we come so far from over de sea,
we heard dat de streets were paved with gold
sometime it hot sometime it cold
I love me mudder and me mudder love me
we try te live in harmony
you might know her as Valerie
but to me she is my mummy.

She shouts at me daddy so loud some time
she don't smoke weed she don't drink wine
she always do the best she can
she work damn hard down ina England,
she's always singing some kind of song
she have big muscles and she very very strong,
she likes pussy cats and she love cashew nuts
she don't bother with no if and buts.

I love me mudder and me mudder love me
we come so far from over de sea
we heard dat de streets were paved with gold
sometime it hot sometime it cold,
I love her and she love me too
and dis is a love I know is true
my family unit extends to you
loving each other is de ting to do.

Benjamin Zephaniah

Large-scale immigration from the West Indies started in the early 1950s. Within a few years there were significant West Indian communities principally in London and Birmingham but also in several other cities. Racial discrimination and downright hostility to West Indians led successive governments in the 1950s and 1960s to introduce controls on immigration and legislation to outlaw racism. There were many immigrants from other parts of the old Commonwealth, such as India, Pakistan and Sri Lanka, and each immigrant group brought to the UK its own culture and traditions, and a richness and variety of life. This poem is by the celebrated West Indian poet, Benjamin Zephaniah, who captures the unusual but beautiful rhythms of West Indian songs in poetry.

1981

A WEDDING SONG

for HRH The Prince of Wales and Lady Diana Spencer
29 July 1981

London Birds: a Lollipop

'Why do those bell-tones crowd the air?'
Cooed the pigeons in Trafalgar Square.

'Because this is the bridal day,'
Said the white swan gliding on Thames broad way.

'Why fire in the sky, when it's meant to be dark?'
Cried the pelican in St James's Park.

'To show that the wedding knot is tied,'
Chirped the Cockney sparrows from Cheapside.

'Who is this couple so fêted and fond?
Quacked the ducks on the Round Pond.

'Our Prince, and England's prettiest flower,'
Croaked an old black raven of the Tower.

John Heath Stubbs

1983

THE FALKLANDS INVASION

Juan Lopez and John Ward

It was their fate to live in a strange time.
The planet had been carved into different countries,
each one provided with loyalties, with loved memories,
with a past which doubtless had been heroic, with
ancient and recent traditions, with rights, with grievances,
with its own mythology, with
forebears in bronze, with anniversaries, with demagogues and
with symbols.
Such an arbitrary division was favourable to war.

Lopez had been born in the city next to the motionless
river; Ward, in the outskirts of the city
through which
Father Brown had walked. He had studied Spanish so as
to read the Quixote.
The other professed a love of Conrad, revealed
to him in a class in Viamonte Street.
They might have been friends, but they saw each other just
once,
face to face, in islands only too well-known,

and each one was Cain, and each one, Abel.
They buried them together. Snow and corruption
know them.
The story I tell happened in a time we cannot
understand.

Jorge Luis Borges
translated from the Spanish by Rodolfo Torragno

In April 1982, General Galtieri, the leader of Argentina, launched a sea and land invasion to reclaim the Falkland Islands, which Argentinians know as Las Malvinas. Within hours troops had occupied the islands and dismissed the British Governor General. Prime Minister Margaret Thatcher decided to send a fleet in order to recapture the Islands – a move that amazed the world. On 25 April, the British fleet recaptured the island of South Georgia and, following a land and sea invasion of the islands, on 14 June British Forces recaptured the capital, Port Stanley. This re-inforced Margaret Thatcher's reputation as the 'Iron Lady' and certainly contributed to her sweeping re-election victory in 1983. This poem was written by the blind Argentinian poet Jorge Luis Borges, who sent it to be published in *The Times* in the hope that it might lead to a better understanding between Britain and Argentina.

Rate-Cap Music

Four hundred arts organisations, including the
English National Opera, the National Theatre, the
London Festival Ballet and London orchestras, are facing
possible extinction because of cuts caused by the
government's rate-capping programme.

It's no go the concert-hall,
It's no go the opera,
All they want is a darkened house
And a corpse cut up by a doctor.
Their pockets are filled with lumps of lead,
Their boots are made for kicking,
Their hearts are lined with frosted glass
And their heads with metal sheeting.

It's no go the council grant,
It's no go the players,

All they want is a nation starved
And robbed of its eyes and ears.

It's no go the soaring voice,
It's no go the dancers,
Say goodbye to the living stage
And the life that art enhances.
The pound is falling hour by hour,
The pound will fall forever,
But if you break their bloody necks,
You won't destroy their ledgers.

Roger R. Woddis

In the early 1980s, the Conservative government tried to reduce the
rising level of town hall expenditure by limiting a council's right to set
its own rate – this was known as rate-capping. Town halls did not like it
and this led to a series of confrontations between local and central
government, the most famous of which was when Liverpool, led by
Derek Hatton, tried to take on the government and lost. Roger Woddis
wrote regular parodies for the *New Statesman*; this one is based upon
Louis MacNeice's famous poem, 'Bagpipe Music'.

1990

The Supporter

If I should be arrested think of me:
That there's some corner of a foreign town
Which is forever Leeds United, we
Got plastered, shouted, fought and then fell down –
Louts whom England bored, made unaware,
Gave, once, her flowers to trample, streets to roam;
Hooligans of England – shaven hair,
Tattooed, flag-swathed – at war away from home.

And think, this hero spoiling for a fight,
And brought up on the wrong side of the fence
Gives somewhere back neglect by England given:
Her slights and wounds; dreams brutal as the night;
A tabloid culture breeding violence
In hearts by patriotic hatred driven.

Simon Rae

England and Scotland in the 1980s built up an unwelcome reputation for football violence and for a time their teams were excluded from European competitions. Margaret Thatcher's attempts to control the violence by compulsory membership of football clubs was abandoned but, more effectively, remote control cameras were placed in and around grounds which reduced the anonymity of the hooligans, and standing terraces were replaced by all-seater stadiums. But, the tendency for a small handful of fans to engage in gratuitous violence did not disappear. In May 1990 some Leeds United supporters rampaged in Bournemouth which prompted Simon Rae to write for the *Guardian* this parody of Rupert Brooke's famous poem, which starts, 'If I should die think only this of me'.

1995

The Minister Has All His Notes in Place
(A poem for Bosnia)

The Minister has all his notes in place.
No line of truth has etched his handsome face.
The House is sparse; they've heard it all before.
His expert lies massage away the war.

While Serbian artillery take aim,
Decide which new civilians they should maim,

He fills the Chamber high with empty talk,
And here's another child will never walk.

The opposition make synthetic rant;
He answers with the Foreign Office cant.
Some random shrapnel takes a boy's right eye:
The other one is all he needs to cry.

'Next business', and the Minister displays
A lapdog urge to hear officials' praise.
A woman fetching water stops a shell.
He smiles: 'That all went over rather well.'

Richard Heller

When Yugoslavia broke up in 1990, a series of savage wars broke out in the Balkans. Neighbours became enemies and a new phrase was coined to describe the ruthless slaughter of minority groups, whether racial, nationalist or religious – 'ethnic cleansing'. The West dithered and the United Nations was ineffective. It was only when NATO forces intervened, to stop further atrocities by the Serbs in Bosnia, that peace negotiations started in earnest. This poem targets the British Foreign Secretary for doing nothing to stop the Serbs.

1997

THE DEATH OF PRINCESS DIANA

Mythology

Earth's axle creaks; the year jolts on; the trees
begin to slip their brittle leaves their flakes of rust;
and darkness takes the edge off daylight, not
because it wants to – never that. Because it must.

And you? Your life was not your own to keep
or lose. Beside the river, swerving underground,
the future tracked you, snapping at your heels:
Diana, breathless, hunted by your own quick hounds.

Andrew Motion

Princess Diana was killed in a car accident in a Paris underpass in the early hours of 30 August 1997 as she and her lover, Dodi Al-Fayed, were trying to escape from the relentless pursuit of the paparazzi. Her death dominated the global media, for she was the most recognizable woman in the world, and it was especially tragic that someone so beautiful should be struck down in her prime. In London, millions of people shared in the public mourning by laying a huge carpet of flowers outside Kensington Palace and Buckingham Palace. It was clear that Diana's death touched many people in a quite unexpected way and little else was talked about in Britain for ten days. A myth was born.

1998

Cool Britannia

'When Britain first at Blair's command
Emerged from years of Tory say,
This was the message (the message) for our land,
To be repeated every day:

Cool Britannia! Britannia cool and bold
Britons never (never, never) shall grow old.

New Labour, be our watchword now;
Old Labour surely got it wrong.
Forward, New Britain (New Britain) take a bow,
And join the chorus of our song:

Cool Britannia! Britannia cool and bold
Britons never (never, never) shall grow old.

                                                      John Marriott

In May 1997, Tony Blair and New Labour decisively defeated John Major and won an overall majority in the House of Commons of 179. New Labour had shrugged off the socialism of old Labour and set as its purpose the modernisation of Britain. The spin-doctors decided to 're-brand' Britain and the phrase 'Cool Britannia' was born to show the way forward. This was a perfect target for the satirists and Tony Blair quietly let it be known that it was not his idea. The *New Statesman*, a supporter of Labour both old and new, ran a competition in April 1998 to devise new words on the theme of 'Cool Britannia' for Thomas Arne's famous patriotic song, 'Rule Britannia'. This was one of the prize-winners.

from Little Gidding, Four Quartets

V

What we call the beginning is often the end
And to make an end is to make a beginning.
The end is where we start from. And every phrase
And sentence that is right (where every word is at home,
Taking its place to support the others,
The word neither diffident nor ostentatious,
An easy commerce of the old and the new,
The common word exact without vulgarity,
The formal word precise but not pedantic,
The complete consort dancing together)
Every phrase and every sentence is an end and a beginning,
Every poem an epitaph. And any action
Is a step to the block, to the fire, down the sea's throat
Or to an illegible stone: and that is where we start.
We die with the dying:
See, they depart, and we go with them.
We are born with the dead:
See, they return, and bring us with them.
The moment of the rose and the moment of the yew-tree
Are of equal duration. A people without history
Is not redeemed from time, for history is a pattern
Of timeless moments. So, while the light fails
On a winter's afternoon, in a secluded chapel
History is now and England.

T. S. Eliot

Acknowledgements

For permission to reprint copyright material the publishers gratefully acknowledge the following:

Faber and Faber Ltd for 'Alas! Poor Queen' from *The Turn of the Day* by Marion Angus (Porpoise Press, 1931); Earl Attlee for 'On Himself' by Clement Attlee; Faber and Faber Ltd for 'September 1, 1939' by W. H. Auden from *The English Auden: Poems, Essays and Dramatic Writings 1927–39*, edited by Edward Mendelson (Faber, 1977), and 'Partition' from *W. H. Auden: Collected Poems*, edited by Edward Mendelson (Faber, 1977), and 'Partition' from *W. H. Auden: Collected Poems*, edited by Edward Mendelson (Faber, 1976); Carcanet Press for 'Mr Dombey' in 'Victorian Trains' from *Collected Poems* by Patricia Beer (Carcanet, 1988); Peters, Frasers & Dunlop Group Ltd for 'On Edward VII' and 'On Bonar Law' by Hilaire Belloc; Curtis Brown Ltd, London, on behalf of the Estate of E. C. Bentley for 'George III' from *The Complete Clerihews of E. Clerihew Bentley* (Oxford University Press, 1981) © the Estate of E. C. Bentley; John Murray (Publishers) for 'The Arrest of Oscar Wilde at the Cadogan Hotel', 'The Death of King George V' and 'In Westminster Abbey' from *Collected Poems* by John Betjeman (John Murray, 1958) and 'Henley Regatta, 1902' from *Uncollected Poems* by John Betjeman (John Murray, 1982); The Society of Authors on behalf of the Laurence Binyon Estate for 'For the Fallen' by Laurence Binyon from *The Times* (September 21, 1914); Carcanet Press for 'Kett's Rebellion' by Keith Chandler; A. P. Watt Ltd on behalf of The Royal Literary Fund for lines from 'The Ballad of the White Horse', 'They said (when they had dined at Ciro's)', 'Elegy in a Country Churchyard' and lines from 'The Secret People' by G. K. Chesterton; the author for 'After Edgehill, 1642' from *Leafburners: New and Selected Poems* by Gladys Mary Coles (Duckworth, 1986); Kevin Crossley-Holland and Rogers, Coleridge and White Ltd for lines from 'The Battle of Maldon' from *The Anglo-Saxon World: An Anthology*, edited and translated by Kevin Crossley-Holland (Oxford University Press, 1984), ©

Kevin Crossley-Holland, 1984; Faber and Faber Ltd for 'The Miners on Strike' by Idris Davies from *The Angry Summer* (Faber, 1943); Faber and Faber Ltd for lines from *Murder in the Cathedral* by T. S. Eliot (Faber, 1935), copyright 1935 by Harcourt Brace Jovanovich, Inc., renewed by T. S. Eliot, and for lines from 'Little Gidding' from *Four Quartets* by T. S. Eliot (Harcourt Brace Jovanovich, Inc. 1935)/*Collected Poems 1909–1962* by T. S. Eliot (Faber, 1963), copyright 1943 by T. S. Eliot, renewed 1971 by Esme Valerie Eliot; Carcanet Press for '1805' from *Complete Poems* by Robert Graves (1995); The Blackstaff Press for 'Christ Goodbye' from *Ruined Pages: Selected Poems* by Padriac Fiacc, edited by Gerald Dawe and Aodan Mac Poilin; Bill Greenwell for 'The Ancient Premier' from *New Statesman* (20 December 1996); Centerprise for 'October 1936' by Milly Harris; Tony Harrison for 'The Morning After' from *Selected Poems* (Penguin Books, 1989); David Higham Associates for 'Great Black-Backed Gulls' from *A Parliament of Birds* by John Heath-Stubbs (Chatto & Windus, 1975) and 'Two Wedding Songs' from *Collected Poems* by John Heath-Stubbs (Carcanet Press, 1988); Faber and Faber Ltd for 'The Martyrdom of Bishop Farrar' from *The Hawk in the Rain* by Ted Hughes (Faber, 1957), ©Ted Hughes, 1957; A. P. Watt Ltd on behalf of The National Trust for Places of Historic Interest or Natural Beauty for 'The Window at Windsor', lines from 'The Female of the Species', 'The Looking Glass', lines from 'The Roman Centurion's Song', 'Danegeld' and 'A Smuggler's Song' from *Selected Poems* by Rudyard Kipling, edited by Peter Keating (Penguin Twentieth-Century Classics, 1993) and 'The Reeds of Runnymede', 'James I' and 'The foundation of Philosophical Doubt . . .' from *Rudyard Kipling's Verse: Definitive Edition* (Hodder & Stoughton, 1940); Faber and Faber Ltd for 'An Arundel Tomb' and 'MCMXIV' from *The Whitsun Weddings* by Philip Larkin (Faber, 1964); Michael Longley for 'Grace Darling' and 'Florence Nightingale', Faber and Faber Ltd for 'Sir Thomas More' from *History* by Robert Lowell (Faber, 1973); David Higham Associates for lines from 'Autumn Journal' from *The Collected Poems of Louis MacNeice* (Faber, 1966); Harold Massingham for his translation of 'The Battle of Brunanburh' from *Frost-Gods* (Macmillan, 1971); Peters, Fraser & Dunlop Group Ltd for 'Mythology' by Andrew Motion from *The Times*; Peter Newbolt for 'Drake's Drum' and 'Vitai Lampada' from *Selected Poems of Henry Newbolt* (Hodder & Stoughton, 1981); Sir Rupert Hart-Davis for 'The Boer War' from *Collected Poems* by William Plomer (Jonathan Cape, 1973); David Higham Associates for 'For Johnny' from *Collected Poems* by John Pudney (Putnam, 1957); George Sassoon for 'The General' from *Collected Poems 1908–1956* by Siegfried Sassoon (Faber, 1961); William Scammell for 'Ancient and Modern' from *Jouissance* (Peterloo Poets, 1985); Macmillan General Books for 'It Did Not Last' from *Collected Poems* by J. C. Squire (Macmillan, 1959); Carcanet Press for 'An Ode for Trafalgar Day' from *Rounding the Horn: Collected Poems* by Jon Stallworthy (Carcanet, 1998); Whitechapel Art Gallery for 'Whitechapel in Britain' by Avram Stencil from the catalogue published on the occasion of the *This is Whitechapel* exhibition (London, 1972) © Avram Stencl and Whitechapel Art Gallery, London; D. M. Thomas for 'Song of the Cornish Wreckers'; Carcanet Press for 'Mr Gradgrind's Country' from *The Collected Poems of Sylvia Townsend Warner*, edited by Claire Hanman (Carcanet, 1982).

Every effort has been made to trace or contact all copyright holders. The publishers would like to apologize to those copyright holders not acknowledged in the above list, and would be pleased to rectify any omissions brought to their notice at the earliest opportunity.

Index of Authors

Index of Titles and First Lines